CHURCH
IN THE
MIDDLE

Stepping outside the building
to reach the world of tomorrow

Rolland Daniels, Ed.D.

D1598021

Published by Warner Press Inc
Warner Press and "WP" logo are trademarks of Warner Press Inc

Church in the Middle
Stepping outside the building to reach the world of tomorrow
Written by Rolland Daniels Ed.D.

Copyright ©2014 Rolland Daniels
Cover, Design, and Layout Copyright ©2014 by Warner Press Inc

Tree 1:3, an imprint of Warner Press, publishes ministry resources designed to help people grow more deeply in their faith.

Requests for information should be sent to:
Warner Press Inc
1201 East Fifth Street
P.O. Box 2499
Anderson, IN 46012
www.warnerpress.org

Editors: Karen Rhodes, Robin Fogle
Cover by Curtis D. Corzine
Design and layout by Curtis D. Corzine

All photos copyright ©Thinkstock and their rightful owners

ISBN: 978-1-59317-738-6

Over fifty years ago, Alvin Toffler's best-seller *Future Shock* predicted that the pace of exponential change would transform western society, upending values, moral boundaries, and traditional institutions long treasured and thought transcendent.

Well, the future is here and the pace of change continues unabated. In a civilization devolving, how does the Church move forward, honoring the living Christ and actually following Him? How does the Church remain true to its Founder, finding the energy, power, and resiliency that propelled it in its beginning?

Rolland Daniels' *The Church in the Middle* paves the way, leading us into life-changing ministry, step by step, helping us refocus on what Jesus came to do in the first place. He did not walk into our world to develop greenhouses into which His followers could retreat; He walked into this world and dwelt among us, meeting us on the streets and in the tough corners of everyday life.

The Church in the Middle is an excellent read that will open your eyes to the promise and power resident in every member of the Body of Christ. **Buy it. Read it. Do it.**

Jim Lyon
General Director, Church of God Ministries, Anderson, Indiana

Special thanks to

my wife, Ellen, and our children,
Tyler, Seth, and Catherine.

You always give me the motivation
and encouragement
to strive for God's best.

Dedicated to Derek Packard,

a young man who will
never be forgotten—
always loved and forever cherished.

TABLE OF CONTENTS

INTRODUCTION

In August 2005, Hurricane Katrina hit land just east of New Orleans. The antiquated levee systems, which were built to protect the city and surrounding areas, were no match for the onslaught of water that the storm surge produced. The Hurricane Protection System for Southeast Louisiana was designed utilizing a traditional approach that was component-performance-based. The tragedy occurred, however, because Katrina was anything but traditional, and the levee systems' design proved to be catastrophic.

In the aftermath of the storm, an Interagency Performance Evaluation Taskforce was created to study and identify the causes of failure and poor performance in order to utilize new knowledge in the repair and reconstruction of the levee system. It was suggested that instead of utilizing the prior traditional approach, a risk-based approach was needed to allow for the explanation of uncertainty where there were multiple integrated components involved (Sills, Vroman, Wahl & Schwanz, 2008.)[1] As a result of the knowledge generated by this study, new design methods are being put into practice and will continue to evolve in order to address the storms that lie ahead.

In some ways, the story of Katrina could be the story of the Western Church. The traditional systems, which guided the establishment of most of our congregations, are being overwhelmed by the storm surge that cultural and generational change has placed upon them. Like the pre-Katrina levee systems, our philosophy and methodology took a performance-based, attractional approach. In like manner, our attractional approach has been slow, unwilling, or unable to respond to the uncertainty that so many changing dynamics have placed upon us. The potential results could be catastrophic for the Kingdom, as a majority of our traditional, attractional congregations have plateaued or are declining, and younger generations are exiting our congregations in mass. In view of these dynamics, perhaps the greater body of Christ should begin to evaluate antiquated systems. Then it should ask if there are fresher methods and philosophies that need to be implemented in order to address the storm surges of the present and future.

WHY THIS BOOK WAS WRITTEN

This book was written in response to that notion. As we look to the future, we must understand that today's world is growing weary of the performance-based philosophy that guides many congregations, and our commitment and dependence upon the brick and mortar structures that house them. The Gospel in the future will be best proclaimed by the compassion and servanthood lived outside those walls, with the love of Jesus. Congregations will be most effective in reaching their communities when they exit their buildings and engage their communities as Jesus did.

I must confess I am deeply moved by the missional church and its leaders. This year I celebrate my thirty-first year in ministry. I have pastored congregations both small and large. My life and calling find their meaning in Kingdom work. Simply put, I love the Church. Yet, deep inside my heart, I believe that unless the church sees ministry differently and engages our communities in a new way, the Kingdom will not influence and impact our culture the way it should. And, the church, as many of us know it, will become more and more irrelevant as we hold on to that which is not working. I have a great fear that if we do not make some seismic shifts in the way we practically live out our faith and intentionally engage our communities with the tangible love of Jesus, we will miss entire generations in the coming decades. For the greater Kingdom's sake, this is a mistake we cannot afford to make.

Church in the Middle was written to enable leaders and congregations to make this journey from attractional to missional living in a constructive and productive manner. In a workbook style, this material will give congregations a six-step process to follow during the journey. My deepest and most sincere hope and prayer is that in the end this information will enable all who read it to experience and live out the Kingdom with greater passion and effectiveness. In doing so we will, by extension, lift up and honor the name and cause of Jesus. There can be no greater goal and purpose for any book than that.

The book is broken down into six chapters, each of which is designed to build on the previous one as leader and congregation make their way beyond the church caught in the middle. At the end of each chapter, a discussion guide is offered. Please note: this process will take time. You could make your way through the process in 6 weeks, but it would probably not be the healthiest of journeys. For Type A personalities like me, this commitment to taking your time will not be easy, but necessary. Let's begin the journey!

LIVING IN THE LAND OF BOTH / AND

Have you ever found yourself in a place or situation in life when you have this epiphany that something needs to change, yet are unsure of exactly what to do? You come to the realization that the way you have been doing things or handling a relationship needs to take a different course if a different outcome is to result. That very moment took place when our oldest son, Tyler, was in the eighth grade. He was experiencing the typical middle school years and was spreading his wings and pushing the limits somewhat. As a result, we seemed to be butting heads at every turn. I personally seemed to be at odds with him more often than not. At that point, our relationship was built more on tension than peace.

Here's the kicker: *I was the problem*. When it comes to personality, Ty and I are opposites. I am a Type A person, who is task-oriented and driven. I like catalytic change and am very comfortable with it. If there are issues, I want to address them soon and come to some resolution. Tyler, on the other hand, is my dad made over. In fact, sometimes we refer to him as Everett, Jr. Trust me, this is a great thing. My dad is the finest man I have ever known, and I wish I were more like him. I am happy to say, Tyler is.

AT THAT POINT OUR RELATIONSHIP WAS BUILT MORE ON TENSION THAN PEACE.

HERE'S THE KICKER:

I WAS THE PROBLEM.

Tyler is laid back and easy going. He never gets too high and never too low. I think that is why he is such a great golfer; nothing on the course alters his approach to the game. He is a processor, does not like great change, and finds great strength and meaning in traditions. The problem with all of this was it didn't coordinate with how I wanted to parent him. Then, one day that all-important moment took place, and I had an epiphany. Okay, the truth is Ellen, my wife, had an epiphany and shared it with me.

Ty and I had just gone through our latest battle. I had pushed too hard and the result was the same—I was angry and tense, and Ty had retreated to his room to escape the drivenness of Dad. Ellen, with great grace, walked up to me and simply said these words, "Rolland, you need to realize Tyler is never going to be you."

Wow, it was as if she had slapped me in the face with this new reality. I immediately understood the problem and a critical truth. I was trying to make Tyler something he was not, and no matter how hard I tried, the same destructive results were going to take place if I didn't change the way I approached our relationship. I took several moments to gather my thoughts. To be honest, I went out on our porch and asked God's forgiveness for the way I had so poorly parented our son. Then I made my way to Tyler's room and asked his forgiveness. I explained what had just taken place and that I wanted to start over. I gathered both our boys, Ty and Seth, in Ty's room and told them that when my Type A personality started coming out too strongly, they had the freedom and my blessing to say, "Chill, Dad," and I would know to back off. A few weeks later, I was at it again and Tyler paused, grinned at me, and said, "Chill, Dad." At that moment we both started laughing, and we started a new beginning.

Over the next few weeks and months, we began reconstructing our relationship. Tyler is a man of few words, except on the golf course. That is his place of comfort and, I believe, his refuge. I started taking one evening a week and playing nine holes of golf with him. Some days, I wouldn't play at all; I would just ride in the golf cart and listen. Today, I have great relationships with the two greatest sons in the world. I owe it all to the moment when God showed me that the way I was relating to my sons had to change.

I believe the same is true in the life of the Western Church today. We stand at a crossroads in our history. Changes in the life of the Church over the past two decades have, in many areas, been at warp speed. Whether it be worship style, the use of media, the concept of missional versus attractional, the erosion of denominational allegiance, satellite congregations, the globalization of the Gospel—change has been a major, continual component of today's Church—and is happening at an exponential clip.

missional
The church has left the building!

attractional
If you build it, they will come.

In many ways, it feels like we are standing on a mountain, watching history being played out in the valley below. For many, the scene is difficult to watch and even more difficult to be a part of. Life as we have known it, particularly within the Western Church, will never be the same. The changing culture that now surrounds us is foreign to many of us. We have not only eclipsed the Post-Modern but now are moving past Post-Christian. Change is always a struggle, but when change affects a part of our DNA, woven into the fabric of our hearts, then *struggle* does not quite define the inner angst that we experience.

There are many reasons for the shifts and transitions taking place within our midst. Perhaps the following historical perspective will help us to understand how different generational viewpoints have helped initiate change in the life of the church.

The story begins follow- ing WWII when the "Greatest Generation," as Tom Brokaw referred to them[2], returned from the war and began doing what they did best: building organizations and institutions. Thus began our country's dominance in the areas of manufacturing and institutional distinction.

So prominent and trust- worthy were these institutions that entire families built their lives and their children's lives and futures around them. Workers spent the lifespan of their working days associated with one company. During this time, they had a plan, showing how many years they would need to work in order to accumulate the benefits and pension necessary for retirement. Then, they would work the plan so that many took early retirement at age 55-60.

The church was a part of this institutional framework. Families were committed to specific denominations and loyal to specific congregations. In many cases, none questioned where their family would attend church; it was just assumed. As a result, multiple generations would follow each other into the familiar pew-lined sanctuaries.

In those days, the church was seen as a bastion of integrity. Truth was spoken, and right and wrong were clearly delineated in the pulpits. Those structures, whether made of brick and mortar or white wooden frames, were seen as institutions that influenced the cultures of their communities.

Today, however, is different. The loyalty to denominations is nonexistent, as doctrinal stances have little influence on the church people choose to attend. Those congregations that once influenced the culture of their communities are now made up of commuters, not community folks. In some ways, our community-mindedness has been replaced by a consumerism that asks what meets our needs, instead of what needs can we help fulfill in our community. Because of these dynamics, our faith is largely relegated to activities lived out within the confines of the walls that house our institutions of faith.

These are just some of the dynamics that are creating the tension developing in the Church today. **Upcoming generations are not drawn to institutions**; they are, in fact, distrustful of them. Before we rush to judgment and declare these future generations unfit to carry our legacies, let's note some of the underlying reasons for their doubts and distrust.

1. The institution of marriage has failed them. More than 50% of all marriages end in divorce. This statistic includes marriages both inside and outside the church. For the children who passed through the dysfunction of divorce, parents, who were supposed to be the constants in their lives, were relegated to non-existent or part-time status. Stability was replaced with brokenness, and trust gave way to distrust. This point is not made to place guilt on those whose lives have been touched by divorce. It is simply shared to illustrate the pain and distrust divorce brings to all involved, particularly the children.

2. The institutional church has had its own troubles. Surrounding the church have been headlines clouded with tales of embezzlement, child abuse, pedophilia, and unwillingness to accept responsibility for wrongs committed. Current generations are not certain if the organized church is really a genuine community of faith or an institution that lives only to protect its existence. They hear about faith, but

see little evidence of how faith makes a difference outside the walls of the church. They witness lifestyles within those walls that look much like the consumer-driven lives they see from those outside the faith. To say the least, these dynamics have caused confusion and disillusionment toward the institutional church.

3. Many of the corporate institutions that once provided this generation's grandparents and parents with occupations and sustenance no longer exist. Our current generation is the most media-savvy of any generation to date. They are quite aware that only a few years ago, some of these same institutions downsized and laid off their parents without any notice. Almost at the same time, the institutions, where their parents and grandparents gave their working lives, dropped or cut significantly their health coverage and, in some cases, pension funds were lost completely. They watched bailouts of banking institutions, which almost took our country under out of pure greed. Lifestyles of incessant debt led to record-setting foreclosures that touched many of their lives in difficult ways. Is it any wonder why this generation will have a tendency to change jobs 9-11 times in a career, or why trust is not given easily to any corporation or organization, including the Church as we know it?

In response to this growing distrust, Dick Hamm writes, That the situation facing the traditional church today is in many ways "the perfect storm."[3] The winds of change have shifted so fast, many congregations have not been able to recalculate their course or reset their sails to effectively navigate the seas at hand. For those of us who have been in ministry for an extensive period of time, we understand all too well this is not the easiest of moments to be in leadership.

Current generations are not certain if the organized church is really a genuine community of faith or an institution that lives only to protect its existence.

TWO PHILOSOPHICAL APPROACHES

In his book, *Missional Renaissance*, Reggie McNeal helps us understand why this dissonance is so prevailing. McNeal reveals there are now two philosophical approaches to how churches operate. The first we call the Traditional View and the second, the Missional View.[4] Those of us born before 1990 will relate immediately to the Traditional View. (The following description will give a sense of familiarity with systems we have grown comfortable with—that have guided our notions of what it meant to do church.) The Missional descriptions may challenge our understanding of church. It is possible that we will sense some commonality with the descriptions used, but are unsure of exactly what it means to live them out as the body of Christ. Therein lies the uncertainty and struggle facing many of our congregations and pastors today.

1. THE TRADITIONAL VIEW

Holy person/priest – serves as intercessor and God's representative for the people

Parish minister/chaplain – caretaker of the Christ followers

Wordsmith/educator – presents the Word correctly

Professional manager – contractual notion of services rendered

Organization – committees/boards with institutional functions

Worship – focuses on the edification and pleasure of the members

Attractional focus – getting people to come to us, brick-and mortar-centered

2. THE MISSIONAL VIEW

Pastor – leader, visionary – articulates a compelling vision that translates the great commission into ministry context

Missional – people sent by God to take the Good News outside the church into the community. The Great Commission: Go is the marching order for congregations

Kingdom conscious – seeks to discover God and join Him, more focused on community than on church agenda. It's all about the Kingdom.

Team players – create teams to accomplish common ministry objectives

Entrepreneurs – intentionally strategize ways to engage those who do not know Jesus

Mentors and supporters – model/walk beside people as they grow into effective missional living

Spiritual – possesses a spiritual presence and energy that is unmistakably that of Jesus and the Holy Spirit at work

Worship – focuses on a "both/and" approach to believers and nonbelievers

THE MISSIONAL CHURCH

"Jesus Christ is the embodiment of that mission;

the Holy Spirit is the power of that mission;

the church is the instrument of that mission;

and the culture is the context

in which that mission occurs."[5]

Ed Stetzer

As we acknowledge the tensions facing the Church today and the changing culture of the ministry, the reality is that most of us function in a dual world. We live and work *in the land of both/and*, while our congregations are *caught in the middle*. The majority of the congregations we currently serve are based on an attractional philosophy. The question that drives and guides our ministries is this: How do we get people to come to our church? The majority of our programs and initiatives are built around discovering ways to answer that question. Sometimes our efforts, energies, and resources have been rewarded with results; however, lately we are discovering that the return on our investments has taken a downturn, and the need to do bigger and better is becoming more and more exhausting. In the end, we wonder if the ability to draw a crowd is really making a Kingdom difference or simply enabling believers to transfer from one church to another.

> **People are no longer moved by brick and mortar, engaged by the production of the big show**

What makes this time even more difficult is that we are entering an age where people are no longer moved by brick and mortar, engaged by the production of the big show, or drawn to the institutions that encompass them. Their hearts are not moved by the hype of attraction; in fact, they are turned off by it. The current generations do not want to *hear* about faith. They want to see, touch, smell, and actively *engage* in their faith. For them, faith is to be lived out as the hands and feet of Jesus in the community where the congregation resides. They do not sense an overwhelming need to bring people to a building as much as they are inclined and impassioned about going to people in need. The Gospel calls them to live out their faith in a missional form. They perceive themselves as sent people who are actively going and engaging folks with the tangible love of Jesus.

Now, here are our dilemmas. First, most pastors who have been in ministry over 10-15 years find themselves ministering to attractional congregations that are financially driven and supported by members who are comfortable and accustomed to this way of life. We may desire to become more missional and reach a younger generation, but realize that transitioning the culture of our congregation will not be an easy or comfortable journey to navigate.

Yet, if truth be told, we also realize, like I did with my son Tyler, that something new needs to happen in the way we relate to people. If our congregation desires to influence our community for the cause of Jesus and have a legacy to pass on in the future, then change is not an option but a *necessity*. If we don't change, we will continue to see younger generations leaving the church and our congregation's legacy eroding as the years pass.

This leads us to our second dilemma. Studies show that most clergy today already feel ill equipped to fulfill their roles. Those leading *caught in the middle* churches do not find themselves in an enviable position. Most of the pastors reading this just said, "Tell us something we don't know." Throw into the mix the changing currents noted previously, and the whole situation facing local congregations and their leadership today seems overwhelming. Many of our congregations and pastors feel paralyzed by the challenges that *the land of both/and* present for them.

The following letter is found in Halter and Smay's book, *The Tangible Kingdom Primer*. The letter reflects the frustration and, in some ways, the sense of failure some pastors feel regarding ministry and moving toward the missional church.

"I didn't go into ministry to be a miserable failure. Frankly, from all my reading, that's pretty much what I gather the younger generations think of us older pastors. I too had dreams of a better day, a larger impact, of better numbers. Can I work harder? No. Can I work smarter? I'm sure I can and that's why I read, listen, seek his face. I'm not complaining or bemoaning my lot.

I wouldn't trade my call for all the world. I just don't think that most of the guys in the missional church movement understand us, or the situations where we find ourselves. The world around us has changed and we didn't change fast enough with it. The jump from modern to postmodern caught us on our heels. Can we still change? I don't know, but we will know soon.

Yes, we often need a kick in the butt (isn't that why we got married?), but we also need a word of encouragement. America would be in [an awful] mess if all the older, traditional type pastors decided to give up, pick up their Bibles, and go home.

Sorry about the acid tone of my response. This is tension, but it's also passion.

Love ya, bro. Go get'em."[6]

The author of the letter describes his frustration toward missional leaders and their perceived lack of understanding regarding the traditional church. Most pastors have experienced this frustration if we have been involved in these types of discussions. Yet, if we are honest and do not internalize the matter, we must admit that a significant portion of our congregations are disconnected from anything or anyone outside our walls. We also recognize this disconnect as our ministries struggle to understand what is needed to engage a changing world. I realize that some peoples' advice at this point would be to move on and let the established church meander its way into oblivion. A prevalent theme in our society today is *forget the church and follow Jesus.*

In some ways, I understand peoples' disillusionment with a segment of the Church. In large part, we have become a group isolated to ourselves. Jesus' words in John 17, "to be in the world but not of the world," have been in many ways neglected.

> "I'm not asking you to take them out of the world, but to keep them safe from the evil one. They do not belong to this world any more than I do. Make them holy by your truth; teach them your word, which is truth. Just as you sent me into the world, I am sending them into the world."
>
> John 17:15-18 (NLT)

Our ministries have been more about us than the communities in which we reside. As stated before, a posture of consumerism and what might be called entitlement have permeated our pews. Please understand: this is not altogether the fault of our people. We have taught them too well to believe the church exists only for them. Because of these dynamics, our faith is largely relegated to activities lived out within the confines of the church walls, and we seldom venture outside. We are more content and comfortable being around other believers than building relationships with nonbelievers, or serving and sharing our faith stories with those outside the faith.

Ultimately, we have convinced ourselves that the Great Commission can be lived out within the walls of our buildings.

THE TRUTH IS IT CANNOT.

In light of all these dilemmas and dysfunction, I still cannot find it within me to ignore or walk away from the traditional church. It has nurtured me and made me who I am in Christ. My great-grandmother helped plant the congregation I was raised in, both physically and spiritually. That is the spiritual legacy from which I come, and it is not within me to abandon it. Nor can I conclude that congregations cannot be transformed through the power of Jesus, just as any individual can. There are too many examples of congregations who through prayer, commitment, hard work, and the Spirit working, have made this difficult transition and transformation.

I AM CONVINCED THAT WE ARE ON THE PRECIPICE OF GREAT KINGDOM RENEWAL AND REVIVAL.

The spiritual hunger found in our world today and the capacity to speak to that hunger through compassion and life engagement is limitless; however, this renewal and awakening will not look, feel, or sound like it always has. Those of us caught in the middle will need new lenses from which to view our ministries and new measuring techniques to replace the old attractional ones.

Because of these issues, I also must acknowledge that not all of us can or will make this journey. Some will just say no. And, as a friend once told me, "I am just going to retire. Every time I think I have a handle on this thing called ministry, someone changes the rules."

Some will see the journey as too demanding, and to be honest, I can understand that. Leadership is exhausting enough without choosing to climb another mountain fraught with slippery slopes. Others will simply ponder the decision to death in an effort to feel spiritual, but in actuality they will end up doing nothing. I am acutely saddened and aware of all these realities.

I am convinced, however, that some will see the great Kingdom potential that awaits the transitioning church. They will determine that the costs are worth the outcome and will commit themselves to do whatever it takes to help transition their congregation to reach a world that is lost and broken.

It is with that belief and intent that this book is offered. The hope is that through extended and intentional journeying together, congregations can move beyond the paralysis in the middle and find themselves in the fruitful land of missional living.

NAVIGATING THE JOURNEY

First, let's begin the missional journey by contemplating three critical questions:

1 Can we bless what is different and encourage what makes us uncomfortable?

If we are honest, most of us have difficulty blessing and encouraging what seems different. But, in reality, this missional journey will not happen until we are willing to move positively toward the future. In our hearts, we must begin to see and believe that the future we are moving toward will be more fruitful than the present we are languishing in.

2 Can we determine to position our congregation to create a positive and productive legacy over the next 5-10 years?

I was discipling a man one time and shared with him some of the necessary changes our congregation would need to make in order to reach a younger generation. He stated that he was really struggling with the changes needed. Then I asked him one simple question, "Do you love your grandchildren enough to make these changes in order to leave them a legacy of your faith?" He responded with a determined look, "Absolutely." Determination is a critical part of this journey. It will not always be easy or comfortable, but we must always be determined to stay the course.

Can we constructively and collectively help move our congregation beyond the obstacles that keep us stuck in the middle?

Notice the two words used to define **how** we make this journey: constructively and collectively. Both are critical factors for a successful journey. "Constructively" entails doing everything within our power not to be destructive. This means enabling the fruit of the Spirit (Galatians 5:22-24) to define characteristics that guide how we treat each other along the way. "Collectively" means we do everything within our power to bring others along. Rest assured, there will be those who choose not to make the journey. This is perfectly okay. It is like any trip—some people choose not to be a part or decide it is not the right destination for them; however, for those who are people-pleasers, any sense that others are not happy will be just cause for aborting the mission. Please don't allow the fixer within you to determine the destination of the whole. Realize that everyone has a choice, and it is not *your* job to make all things perfect.

If you answered these questions in the affirmative, you have taken the first step toward a transformational journey—one that will enable you and your congregation to leave a great legacy for the future. Let's move forward!

CONGREGATIONAL ASSESSMENT

It is productive for all congregations to do periodic assessments. This process enables us to better determine where we are, what some of our obstacles might be, and how we need to proceed. As you make your way through the assessment, review the two philosophical approaches offered by McNeal, on pages 8 and 9, and honestly assess where the different dynamics fit your congregation.

On a scale of 1-10, where would your congregation be and why?

Traditional 1—2—3—4—5—6—7—8—9—10 Missional

_____

_____

_____

_____

_____

It is important to speak openly about our emotions. At some point, those emotions will come out and could derail the initiative to move forward. Why not honestly talk through your concerns up front and move through those emotions and fears together. We all have them, but we can overcome them together.

As you read the opening chapter:

What frustrated you? _____
_____

What confused you? _____
_____

What drained you? _____
_____

What angered you? _____
_____

What excited you?_____
_____

What gave you hope? _____
_____

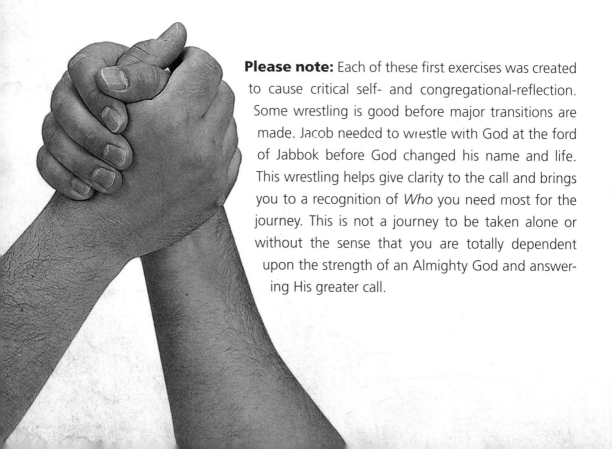

Please note: Each of these first exercises was created to cause critical self- and congregational-reflection. Some wrestling is good before major transitions are made. Jacob needed to wrestle with God at the ford of Jabbok before God changed his name and life. This wrestling helps give clarity to the call and brings you to a recognition of *Who* you need most for the journey. This is not a journey to be taken alone or without the sense that you are totally dependent upon the strength of an Almighty God and answering His greater call.

DEFINING
MISSIONAL

This reality faces us on this journey: There are no experts on transitioning from traditional to missional. Every congregation is different, and the context within and surrounding that congregation is unique and complex. Therefore, one size does not fit all, and no one method or singular game is before us.

It is imperative, however, that a congregation has a clear understanding of where they are headed and what they want to become. The Mad Hatter told Alice, "If you don't know where you are going, any road will get you there." [7]

Through the marketing research that Warner Press did for this book, it became quite clear that many people struggle with a clear understanding of what a missional church is. For that reason, this section initially takes the reader through a process of defining what the term missional means for a congregation.

Also included within this chapter are some potential obstacles and critical insights that must be understood if the journey toward missional is to be made in a productive manner. I am certain each congregation will discover other obstacles and insights as the journey is traversed. We always forget something critical when packing for a trip; this trip will be no different. Remember, every congregation is unique and the dynamics in and around that congregation are unique also. For that reason, the course charted for each individual congregation will need to be customized to fit that particular congregation.

...a community of faith that primarily directs its ministry focus outward toward the neighborhood in which it is located, and to the broader world beyond

DEFINING MISSIONAL

As we begin charting a course, defining the destination we are moving toward might be helpful. Many people do not understand fully what a missional congregation is, and what it is not. Some people define their congregations as missional by the simple fact that they have a missions program within their church. That is not what we are talking about. Some of us are confused already! Because of that confusion, let's take some time to distinguish (differentiate between) what makes a missional congregation, as opposed to a traditional/attractional one.

Leadership Journal, (Fall, 2008) defined a missional congregation as a community of faith that primarily directs its ministry focus outward toward the neighborhood in which it is located, and to the broader world beyond. That local body sees this focus as both its central mission and the organizing principle upon which it functions. Within that community is a deep belief that its missional direction is patterned after what God has done in Jesus Christ. In the incarnation, God sent His Son to a broken and lost world. Similarly, to be missional means to be sent into the world. The missional congregation does not expect people to come to them, but their primary functions are to be "sent people," who enter their context (environment) for the cause of Jesus. It is this intent "to go" that differentiates a missional church from an attractional one. [8]

This missional theology applies to the whole life of every believer. A follower of Jesus is to be a sent agent of the Kingdom of God, and every believer is to carry the mission of God into every sphere of life. Every follower of Christ is called to function as a missionary sent into a non-Christian culture. Certainly, missional represents a significant shift in the way we think about the church. As the people of an incarnate Lord, whose all-encompassing love compelled Him to engage our broken world, we ought to engage the world the same way. We are called to "go to" rather than to ask people to come to us.

A critical question is this: How does a congregation fulfill the declarations of a missional church? In the book, *Breaking the Missional Code*, David Putman and Ed Stetzer reflect on the following five traits that missionaries practice, regardless of the context.

HOW DOES A CONGREGATION FULFILL THE DECLARATIONS OF A MISSIONAL CHURCH?

First, missionaries study and learn the language of their environment. This seems so practical for a missionary, but in reality it is also practical for a local congregation. We have our own language in the church. Say phrases like "washed in the blood" and "crucified with Christ" outside our walls, and people have very little understanding of what we are talking about. Language is that common denominator that allows us to communicate on a common plane. God understood this on the day of Pentecost when the Holy Spirit came and allowed folks to proclaim the Good News in languages different from their native ones. We as God's people must learn to communicate in the language of the context in which we minister. If not, we might be speaking, but few people are understanding.

Second, missionaries immerse themselves within the culture where they have chosen to reside. Jesus spoke of being sent into the world, but not of the world. Christ's incarnation made evident the fact that He understood the war will never be won inside the fort. To make a Kingdom difference, a congregation must commit themselves to engage the culture where they live. No missionary enters a community and then resolves to have nothing to do with it. To make an eternal difference, we must choose to engage and connect with the people who live in our community.

Third, missionaries proclaim the good news in intentional and creative ways after establishing credibility through relationships. I have often found that many believers function in one of two ways. They are either like secret agents in their work places and neighborhoods, or they are so salty in their presentation of Jesus no one can stand the taste. In either case, they are not very intentional or effective in reflecting Jesus to those outside the faith. Missionaries realize that trust and credibility are keys to effectively sharing Jesus with those who don't know Him. They spend time building both trust and credibility in order to earn the right to have personal conversations related to faith.

Fourth, missionaries are intentional about becoming a consistent presence for the cause of Christ in their communities. Missionaries work to establish an ongoing presence, which allows them to reflect the incarnate Jesus as the hands and feet of Christ. People are more open to hear the Good News when they have first witnessed the love of Jesus that accompanies His Good News. That type of consistent presence enables the Good News to be shared with a power that touches lives more deeply. Missional congregations understand that nothing, absolutely nothing, replaces the power of presence.

Finally, the missionary over time contextualizes biblical life and reflects the reality of Jesus for their culture. I believe this is one of the hardest concepts for the church in the United States to grasp. And it is for this reason we are still functioning under the assumption that we live in a culture that predominantly favors Christianity and carries with it an understanding of what the church is. Please understand—the culture surrounding us does not. [9]

I pastor in a small city called Anderson, Indiana. It is located just 20 miles outside Indianapolis and finds itself in the middle of Midwest values and rural America. An article (Doyle, 2011) in our local newspaper informed its readers that studies revealed seven out of ten Anderson residents have never been to church and eight out of ten have not been to church in the last year.[10] Trust me when I say that the church's influence within our communities is waning. That is why other faith bodies are sending more and more missionaries to our country. Christianity's influence on our culture is declining and other religions are finding open doors to share their message. It has never been more important that local congregations contextualize biblical life, and reflect the tangible reality of Jesus for the communities in which they reside.

MISSIONAL CONGREGATIONS

- **Are incarnational** *(the tangible hands and feet of Jesus)*

- **Are indigenous** *(live, work and minister within the context)*

- **Are intentional** *(are a sent people that go into the world)*[11]
  (Stetzer & Putman)

POTENTIAL OBSTACLES

As we read and define what it means to be missional, we recognize the inner discord this information can create. This dissonance reflects the potential obstacles that could hinder our progression on this journey. These are obstacles that must be named, addressed, and worked through in order to make our way forward.

Obstacle # 1: What we have already learned

"It is impossible for a man to learn what he thinks he already knows." Epictetus

Alan Hirsch (2012) [12]

I enjoy playing golf. The only problem is, I am not very good at it. That is difficult for me, because in days gone by I was a fair athlete. What I find most difficult in my golf game is transitioning from a baseball swing to a golf swing. You would think one would work for the other; however, that is not the case. When I tee off, golfers in fairways nearby have found their location to be hazardous. I learned to swing a baseball bat as a young child and played the sport in an organized manner beginning at age 5. I did not seriously take up golf until later in my adult life. My problem is trying to unlearn what I have already learned. My golf game will attest that it is truly a difficult thing to do!

In the same way, all of us have preconceived notions of what we know regarding the church. For many of us, this knowledge has been passed down from previous generations, and that is certainly not a bad thing. This can, however, create challenges as we attempt to open our minds and hearts to new ways of understanding the church and how God might want to do a new thing in its life. At some point, we must take hold of the Apostle Paul's instruction in Romans 12:2 (NLT), *"Don't copy the behavior and customs of this world, but let God transform you into a new person by changing the way you think."* For most of us, the missional church is a fresh way of perceiving the church. In all actuality, it is simply returning to a New Testament concept; however, before we can embrace it, we must open our minds and hearts to understand and experience a new way of doing ministry.

Obstacle # 2: How we picture the church

"God is always bigger than what we think we know." A.W. Tozer

Alan Hirsch (2012) [13]

My father always told me that perception is 90% of reality. This means that how we see something in our minds is how we perceive it to be in real life. The truth is that reality has been painted for us over time by prior experiences and thoughts. When I did research for my dissertation, I interviewed people regarding their diversity experiences. I was amazed at how their preconceptions of people different from themselves had been established by what they had read, seen on television, or heard from others. I was even more amazed at how those preconceptions changed when they had personal encounters that proved their old biases and prejudices to be false.

In Isaiah 43:18-19 (NIV1984), God instructs us with these words, *"Forget the former things; do not dwell on the past. See, I am doing a new thing! Now it springs up; do you not perceive it? I am making a way in the desert and streams in the wasteland."* God is indeed doing something new in the life of His church. It will not look or function necessarily in the way we think it should. But, if we will open our minds and hearts to the new things He is doing, new ways and methods of being God's sent people will present themselves. I also believe new ways of reaching and engaging our communities for the sake of Christ will emerge.

Obstacle # 3: The fear of the unknown

"We all have a fear of the unknown; what one does with that fear will make all the difference in the world." Lillian Russell [14]

The fear of the unknown is one of the most powerful forces in the world. That fear can keep a man from asking out the girl of his dreams or applying for the job he has wanted for a lifetime. Our need for the common or familiar affects so many aspects of our lives. Even heart transplant patients deal with this struggle. After a heart transplant, the body's desire is to reject what is not common or familiar. Think about that: our body's tendency is to reject what will ultimately save it and restore life to it.

Might it be the same with our spiritual hearts? Can our need for the common and familiar hinder what will ultimately enable our congregations to make a Kingdom difference? Can our comfort zone take precedent over what will give our congregation a spiritual legacy for future decades? In many congregations, the need for personal comfort has overridden the notion that we are called to serve others with Christ's selfless love.

Serving the less fortunate or investing in our communities will always include unknown risks. Within these realms, there are dynamics we will not control and certainly will not be comfortable with. Those circumstances will direct us to depend on the

Sovereign hand of God to intervene and the Holy Spirit to lead, as we allow Him to determine our way. Yet, it is in these arenas that we ultimately fulfill Jesus' challenge of servanthood, given to us in Matthew 20:26-28 (NLT), *"But among you it will be different. Whoever wants to be a leader among you must be your servant, and whoever wants to be first among you must become your slave. For even the Son of Man came not to be served but to serve others and to give his life as a ransom for many."* Servanthood will always call us to confront our fears of the unknown. *Who* we are to serve and *how* we are to serve will always require trust and faith as we ask God to use us in the community where we live.

"The appropriate response to the emerging world is a rebooting of the mission, a radical obedience to an ancient command, a loss of self rather than self-preoccupation, concern about service and sacrifice rather than concern about style."

Reggie McNeal (2003) [15]

Critical Insights

Just as there are obstacles we must name and overcome, there are also insights we must grasp and utilize during our journey. Like a flashlight, these insights can be very handy tools when traveling a dimly lit, unfamiliar path. The key, however, is making certain we take the flashlight out of the drawer and remember to turn it on. Otherwise, the flashlight, like these insights, has great potential but very little use.

Insight # 1: Tradition should be honored, but not worshiped

For every congregation, long-term traditions have been mistakenly idolized over time. This does not minimize their contribution to a congregation's past and present. Some traditions have been worshiped and clung to as having biblical status, when, in reality, they are traditions that at one time were more relevant than they are currently. With these thoughts in mind, we must determine what traditions should be honored, but not see them as non-negotiables on the path to transformation.

It is important to discuss traditions openly. When congregations try to dismiss traditions without thought and dialogue, destruction and conflict usually ensue quickly. Take the time to honor, talk through, and give proper recognition to what has been valued.

Some members of the congregation will experience grief in this time of transition. During my childhood, my family moved to a new home. I remember that my mother cried several times during our relocation. That did not mean she didn't see our new home as very positive, viable, and necessary. It simply meant that we were leaving something very valued behind, and grief was a part of her journey. It will be the same for many in any congregation that goes through culture transition. Make certain not to run roughshod over people's feelings, but listen, be caring, and allow grief to take its natural course.

Even in her grief, Mom understood that our move was necessary to bring about the future she and Dad desired for their children. The same is true for every member who makes up a congregation. **At some point, we must believe that our future is worth moving toward, and that the price we must pay to get there is worth the cost.** Hebrews 12:1-2 (NIV1984) speaks to this, *"Let us throw off everything that hinders and the sin that so easily entangles, and let us run with perseverance the race marked out for us."* Sometimes what entangles a congregation most is the traditions of the past. At some point, we must move ahead to the new thing God is doing and move beyond the past. If not, we, like the Israelites who died in the desert, will never see the Promised Land God has for us.

Insight # 2: Missional does not mean *same*

Most have heard the statement, "No two snowflakes are alike." The same can be said for congregations. No two congregations are the same. Every congregation has a different personality and is attended by people with differing gifts. Congregations are located in different environments, which present different ministry opportunities. As a congregation begins to view its community as a mission field, it must ask two vital questions:

Where can our congregation have the greatest influence for the Kingdom?

Every community has multiple opportunities to serve and meet needs. Every congregation will have folks who have many ideas about where that might be. It is important that congregations not try to be everywhere, but focus on the ministry that allows them the most effectiveness in their efforts. This decision will probably take research, involve success and failure, and ultimately depend on your congregation's willingness to step forward. No congregation can do everything, but every congregation can do something. Determine where your congregation can have the greatest Kingdom influence and then do what you need to do to have a continual presence there.

Who can I personally touch, care for, and influence for the cause of Jesus?

Just as congregations have multiple opportunities for Kingdom influence, so do the individuals who make up those congregations. In chapter 5 we will focus in more detail on how individuals can see the difference their daily lives make for the Kingdom. Most people overlook the multiple opportunities that come their way, which is easy to do since we have been taught that our ministries take place within the walls of the building.

Again, missional does not mean *same*. Each congregation must be free to chart its own course of ministry. No congregation or person is called to be like another, nor should it try to replicate the ministry of Congregation A or Congregation B. Every congregation is unique, and so is its call to mission and ministry. As a congregation, take time to define who you are, what your gifts are, and where you can make the greatest difference for Jesus.

Insight # 3: Transition takes time

There are no quick fixes or overnight solutions to any congregation's transition from attractional to missional. Simply put, the journey takes time. For the traditional congregation to make this transition in a healthy manner could take as long as 3-5 years. Some may take longer, but most will not be shorter. Determine in your mind that this will be a marathon, not a sprint. God's Word speaks specifically to us about staying the course and finishing the race.

Philippians 3:13-14 (NLT), *"I focus on this one thing: Forgetting the past and looking forward to what lies ahead, I press on to reach the end of the race and receive the heavenly prize for which God, through Christ Jesus, is calling us."*

TRANSITION TIPS FOR LEADERSHIP

Be singular in your focus. There are many roads a congregation can choose to travel and many potential detours along the way. Make certain you stay on the roads that lead toward missional transformation. The Apostle Paul said it best in Philippians 3:13 (NLT), "*I focus on this one thing.*" Focus on the goal of enabling your congregation to make this transition in a positive manner.

Stay long enough to complete the journey. One of the critical components of a successful journey is consistency in the leadership position. **It is hard to stay the course when the course keeps changing.** Not many football teams win the big game if they change offensive coordinators every year. Stay long enough to build the credibility and trust necessary to lead your people toward a desired goal.

Develop and work the plan. On critical journeys, it is especially important to know where you're headed. When you board an airplane, don't you hope the crew has a flight plan? Your congregation deserves and desires the same. Chapter 3 will give instructions on utilizing a system called the Root Cause Analysis. Reaching a final destination is so much easier when you have some idea of where you're going. Remember, work to develop a plan and then work the plan.

Celebrate along the way. One weakness of many congregations is the lack of celebration. Take time on this journey to celebrate even the smallest of accomplishments. Honor people who have contributed to reaching the destination and share their stories. Stories have great power to unite, encourage, and embolden people. Joy, laughter, and celebration are critical components for productive teams. Make certain each of these three is felt, heard, and experienced during your journey.

Develop a Congregational Covenant. Come together as a congregation and submit to the following five intentions during the journey. If you do so, the journey will not be perfect (change never is), but the outcome can be productive rather than destructive. That is the ultimate goal. Please, do not allow this important moment to be a casual occurrence or a common event. Make this a moment when the Divine is invited to seal these commitments, and the congregation senses the importance of entering into this covenant together.

TRANSITION

CONGREGATIONAL COVENANT

We will always walk toward each other in grace, not away from each other in anger.

Ephesians 4:3 (NIV1984), *"Make every effort to keep the unity of the Spirit through the bond of peace."*

We will listen, pray, and ponder before we speak or act.

Ephesians 4:29 (NIV1984), *"Do not let any unwholesome talk come out of your mouths, but only what is helpful for building others up according to their needs, that it may benefit those who listen."*

Everyone must be willing to give up something for the good of the whole.

Ephesians 5:21 (NIV1984), *"Submit to one another out of reverence for Christ."*

In all situations, we will strive to be Christlike.

Ephesians 4:32 (NIV1984), *"Be kind and compassionate to one another, forgiving each other, just as in Christ God forgave you."*

We will stay the course and refuse to quit until we reach the chosen destination.

Hebrews 12:1-2 (NLT), *"And let us run with endurance the race God has set before us. We do this by keeping our eyes on Jesus, the champion who initiates and perfects our faith."*

As you make this journey, continually strive to better know the One who is leading you and how He desires you to love others in His name. Then, above all else realize this: The One who guides and calls you put all the stars in place. The Bible even tells us that He knows the stars by name. Rest assured, His hands are big enough to carry you through to His chosen destination.

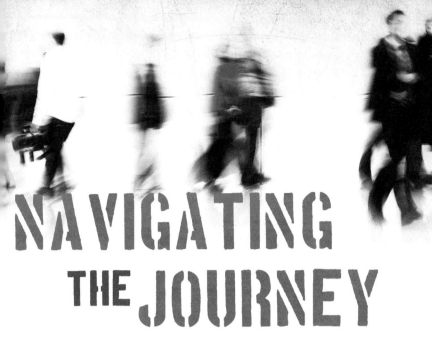

NAVIGATING
THE JOURNEY

Defining Missional

List five traits that distinguish and define the missional church:

1._____

2._____

3._____

4._____

5._____

Check the box for each statement that currently describes your congregation.

☐ We are a missional church because we are a collection of missional believers, acting together to fulfill the mission of God.

☐ We are a missional church because we are a people exploring and rediscovering what our identity and vocation are as Jesus' sent people.

☐ We are a missional church because we are a faith community, willing and ready to be Christ's people in our own situation and place.

☐ We are a missional church because we know that we must be cross-cultural missionary people (contextual), and adopt a missionary stance in relation to our community.

☐ We are a missional church because we will be engaged with the culture (in the world) without being absorbed by the culture (not of the world). [16]

Alan Hirsch, 2012

Which statements will stretch your congregation the most and why?

_____

_____

_____

_____

_____

_____

_____

_____

OBSTACLES

Obstacle #1: What we have already learned

Obstacle #2: How we picture the church

Obstacle #3: Fear of the unknown

Review the obstacles above and list them in the order of difficulty for you or your congregation.

1._____

2._____

3._____

How will you best address and work through obstacles in order to make your way forward?

_____

_____

_____

_____

_____

_____

_____

_____

INSIGHTS

Insight #1: Tradition should be honored, but not worshiped

Insight #2: Missional does not mean *same*

Insight #3: Transition takes time

Which insights helped you the most?

_____

_____

_____

_____

_____

What additional insights will help your congregation better navigate this journey?

_____

_____

_____

_____

_____

_____

CONGREGATIONAL COVENANT

We will always walk toward each other in grace, not away from each other in anger.

"Make every effort to keep the unity of the Spirit through the bond of peace."
Ephesians 4:3 (NIV1984)

We will listen, pray, and ponder before we speak or act.

"Do not let any unwholesome talk come out of your mouths, but only what is helpful for building others up according to their needs, that it may benefit those who listen."
Ephesians 4:29 (NIV1984)

Everyone must be willing to give up something for the good of the whole.

"Submit to one another out of reverence for Christ."
Ephesians 5:21 (NIV1984)

In all situations, we will strive to be Christ-like.

"Be kind and compassionate to one another, forgiving each other, just as in Christ God forgave you."
Ephesians 4:32 (NIV1984)

We will stay the course and refuse to quit until we reach the chosen destination.

"And let us run with endurance the race God has set before us. We do this by keeping our eyes on Jesus, the champion who initiates and perfects our faith."
Hebrews 12:1-2 (NLT)

Signature_____ Date_____

CHANGING THE CULTURE

A delicate balancing act

When any congregation moves from attractional to missional, the current culture that guides that congregation will change. Most who have served in ministry understand what a delicate and difficult balancing act this transition can be. I have always heard that the punch you don't see knocks you out; therefore, it is important that we are honest and upfront regarding the reality of the journey ahead. It will take intentionality, persistence, the right leadership, an effective process, and a great deal of prayer covering for the transition to succeed.

We must not take for granted that pastors/leaders have a second sense about how to lead a congregation or organization through culture change. Many times we assume pastors and congregational leaders are equipped with such knowledge; most are not. Books on cultural change and organizational transformation are not the genre pastors usually read, nor have they been trained in those leadership principles. This is not a criticism, but simply a fact; however, it is a fact that cannot be overlooked on this journey.

Therefore, the Root Cause Analysis model is offered as an option for congregations to follow and to use as a guide. It is not a perfect model, nor is it fail-proof. There are no perfect models at anyone's disposal. But, this model has been utilized by multiple organizations to transition from one destination toward a more desired one. People on a journey need a roadmap, and the Root Cause Analysis can assist a congregation in charting an intentional course.

It will be best utilized if the lead pastor and leadership team pull together a transition team made up of individuals with differing, but necessary gifts. As in any systems approach, the sum of the parts ends up being greater than the whole. It is imperative the critical parts be brought together to work toward the desired whole.

ROOT CAUSE ANALYSIS

While completing his Doctorate of Ministry, Marshall Stokes wrote his dissertation on the utilization of a root cause analysis within a congregational setting, to bring about needed change. The congregation he pastored was stagnant and needed to move outside of themselves. Marshall drew from his extensive business background and realized that a root cause analysis could be transferred to his congregational situation. In doing so, his congregation was able to process through a set of intentional steps that brought about cultural transformation. He graciously allowing his work to be shared in this book in an effort to provide other pastors/congregations a model of culture transformation to work from.[17] (Stokes, 2009)

First, let's better understand what a root cause analysis is. Root cause analysis is a focused, quality improvement tool used to identify the root cause of a problem or adverse occurrence, in order to move an organization in a more positive direction. The goals of a root cause analysis are to provide a true understanding of a problem and to subsequently develop a plan to move beyond the adverse effect of it. Utilizing the root cause process to identify a problem is a reactive approach to solving the problem. The process, however, might also be used as a proactive means of avoiding pitfalls in the process.

Oftentimes, congregations are unaware that their current processes or strategies are ineffective. One major advantage of using a root cause analysis within a local con-gregation is its non-punitive nature. In other words, this tool focuses on processes, not people. This characteristic elicits openness and honesty as the process unfolds. Congregations might not realize, for example, that the "root cause" of a problematic event or status is process-related and not people-related. At the heart of the root cause analysis is a determined effort to discover and understand the cause of an error, not *who* caused the error.

As the congregation enters the process, a root cause analysis assesses a congregation's current state as compared to the desired future state. Both the current and desired states are identified by the congregants in the exercise. Toward this end, participants define the current situation through objective data (numerical and otherwise, such as financial records and attendance records) and not opinions. Next, the congregation strives to articulate and agree on what the future, desired state will look like. After the current and future desired states have been defined, causes are identified that contribute to the present current state and serve as barriers to achieving the desired future state. Finally, actions and strategies are identified to begin bridging the two states. These actions are intended to improve the effectiveness of the process while moving the Church toward the desired destination. An example of a root cause analysis six-step template is offered below, followed by an example of a completed template.

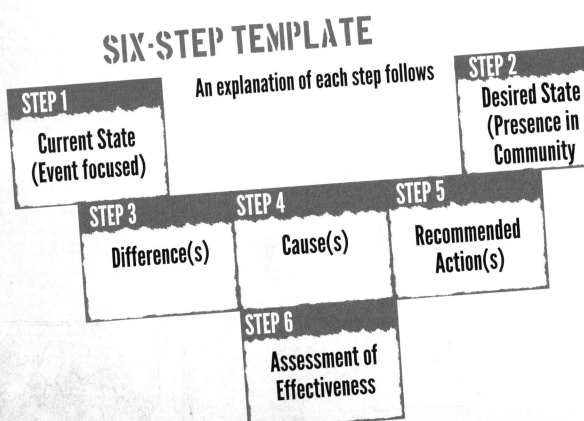

SIX-STEP TEMPLATE

An explanation of each step follows

STEP 1
Current State
(Event focused)

STEP 2
Desired State
(Presence in
Community

STEP 3
Difference(s)

STEP 4
Cause(s)

STEP 5
Recommended
Action(s)

STEP 6
Assessment of
Effectiveness

STEP 1 - CURRENT STATE

Where are we now?

What do our initiatives and numbers tell us?

STEP 2 - DESIRED STATE

What is our desired destination as a congregation?

STEP 3 - DIFFERENCES

What are the noted differences between our current state
and our desired state?

STEP 4 - CAUSES

What are the identified causes that contriute to the present current state
and serve as barriers to achieving the desired future state?

STEP 5 - RECOMMENDED ACTIONS

What actions and strategies are needed to begin to bridge the two states
and move our congregation toward the desired goal?

STEP 6 - ASSESSMENT OF EFFECTIVENESS

Define what measurements, methods, and time will be used to assess
each of our actions and strategies.

How effective have our actions and strategies been in moving
our congregation toward the desired goal?

EXAMPLE OF COMPLETED TEMPLATE

This completed template is a bare-bones, basic terminology approach to each section. Please know that each step must be thoroughly fleshed out in order to be an effective exercise. A word of caution: do not be too quick in moving through each step, but take the necessary time to process each step in a thorough manner.

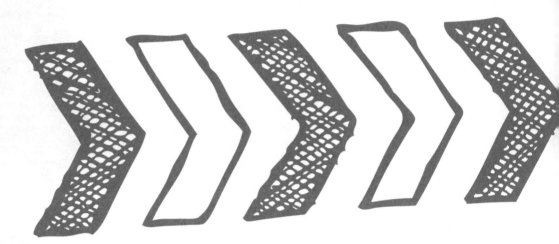

Cogent:
* pertinent
* relevant
* valid
* convincing

The root cause template offered on the next page serves as a framework that enables congregations to understand and identify intangible processes in a tangible way. A root cause analysis can never substitute for a divine work of God, but it can provide a means to view processes tangibly so as to identify opportunities for improvement and cogent strategies for continued spiritual health.

Finally, success or failure of a root cause exercise is heavily dependent on the following: 1) buy-in from leadership; 2) assigning responsibility and target completion dates for each action identified; and, 3) enthusiasm within the leadership base toward cultivating a culture of continuous improvement and involvement.

A root cause analysis can be an extremely helpful tool for any congregation seeking to improve its overall engagement and intentional service to a community because data is hard to argue.

STEP 1

Current State (Event)

Inward, Self-Focused Church

STEP 2

Desired State (Non-Event)

Missional, Community-Oriented Church

STEP 3

Difference(s)

Inward Church	Missional Church
1-Little or no concern for those outside the walls	1-Increasing care and outreach ministries
2- Decreased community involvement	2- Increased community involvement
3-Internal focus on ministries and programming	3-Balanced focus on ministries and programming

STEP 4

Cause(s)

1a-No structured outreach plan

1b-No intentional relationships with those outside the walls

2a- Lack of ownership and proactive action by team leaders

2b-Lack of training offered by leadership

3a-Initial lack of pastoral leadership

3b-Rejection of the leadership's attempts to demonstrate the existence of a problem

3c-General teaching and preaching about the need for change, yet no detailed plan for change offered

STEP 5

Recommended Action(s)

Responsibility: Pastor and Leadership

1-Develop a detailed plan for restructure and re-vitalization of community involvement

2-Endorse the plan and authorize its implementation

3-Offer key, visionary & intentional leadership and training to the congregation

STEP 6: ASSESSMENT

Monitor	September 2014 (Baseline State Prior to Implementation of Action Plan)	September 2015 (Six-Month Review of Post-Implementation)
Average monthly Sunday morning worship service attendance	70	105
Percentage of outreach focused ministries	5	40
Percentage of laity involved outside the walls	10	40
Number of baptisms	2	8
Structure of ministries	Imbalanced	More balanced
Inward/Outward Focus	Imbalanced	More balanced

BUILDING A CULTURE THROUGH SPIRITUAL FORMATION

As we move a congregation toward a missional mindset and heart, certain common denominators should be intentionally established within the culture of that congregation. As we research and share with other congregations on this journey, we find recurring factors that are constant parts of the equation. One of those common denominators is discipleship/spiritual formation. The following quotes show the importance that discipleship/spiritual formation play in this journey:

"When considering what it will take for an existing congregation to move in a missional direction, I believe one of the key starting points is to begin with discipleship, or spiritual formation. Now having said that, I also believe we have to be careful not to think it is a purely linear process. In other words we need to realize that we can't, or shouldn't, see discipleship as something that has to be 'complete' before we engage in God's mission. I would much rather view the process as a cycle of discipleship and mission, where intentional apprenticeship to Jesus (discipleship) leads to mission and mission compels us to intentional apprenticeship (discipleship). The main point that I want to make here, however, is that we cannot neglect the formation to Christlikeness if we are to be a sent, missionary people."[18] (Brad Briscoe, MissionalChurchNetwork.com/ May, 2010)

"God calls the church to be a sent community of people who no longer live for themselves but instead live to participate with Him in His redemptive purposes. However, people will have neither the passion nor the strength to live as a counter cultural society for the sake of others if they are not transformed by the way of Jesus. If the church is to "go and be" then we must make certain that we are a Spirit formed community that has the spiritual capacity to impact the lives of others." [19] (Brad Briscoe, Missional Church Network, May, 2010)

As a congregation approaches this transition toward being missional, the people must begin to see themselves as "sent" people. Here's the kicker: sent people have a deep understanding of their faith and why it compels them to get outside their walls. Spiritual formation is an intentional effort to lay a faith foundation across a congregation that includes crucial elements of a missional mindset and heart. David Kinneman once said, "In our country, we in the church have become christianized, but few have become followers of Jesus"[22] (2012). Discipleship is an intentional effort to create a culture where followers of Jesus are the norm, and their lives are lived out as God's sent people.

Let's take a short quiz:

Think of all the sermons you have listened to, the classes and Bible studies you have attended, the small groups you have been a part of. Now, answer these questions.

How many people have you shared Jesus with in the past 2-5 years?

How many people have you served outside the walls of the church?

How many folks outside the faith have you intentionally built relationships with?

I have an idea most wouldn't receive a passing grade on that quiz. It is puzzling why congregations today are not more involved outside the walls of the church building. Over time and through experience, the following simple truths have brought clarity for me....

PEOPLE CAN'T GIVE AWAY WHAT THEY DON'T OWN.

If faith is not owned in a very personal and intimate way, one can go through life and not see the great value in the faith we claim. Faith is not simply a component of who we are, but something that compels us toward action. It is like the hidden treasure and the pearl of great value described in Matthew 13. The people who found them were compelled to sell all they had in order to purchase them. They had a deep sense of the value that was represented through them. When you own your faith in that manner and, more importantly, when your faith owns you, your life will take on new meaning and direction as you become a sent person, called to help reconcile and transform the world for the cause of Christ. That which you hold in your heart is seen as too valuable to be kept in your heart. You will be compelled to share and serve others in the name of that treasure. This type of ownership only happens if our lives are transformed by the life and example of Jesus.

In reality, the key to this endeavor is for the "sent" person to be in possession of a missional heart fixed on Jesus. If not, he or she will share knowledge, but not a passion for taking faith outside the walls. This missional heart must be shared throughout the process. Repetition is the key—the need to take faith outside the walls must be communicated over and over. Without this emphasis, it is too easy to believe we are growing in our faith for ourselves, and we fail to comprehend that we are growing in order to serve and share with others through our faith.

PEOPLE CAN'T DO WHAT THEY DON'T KNOW.

I read a survey a few years back that stated the number one reason believers gave for not sharing their faith was they didn't know what to say. In essence, we really don't have a working or conversational knowledge of our faith. Please know I am not trying to lay guilt on folks that sit in our pews or those who pastor them. The point is that if we desire our people to engage the world for Christ's sake, then we should enable them to understand their faith and give them the tools to share their faith story.

Read the Apostle Paul's words found in 2 Corinthians 5:14-20 (NIV1984).

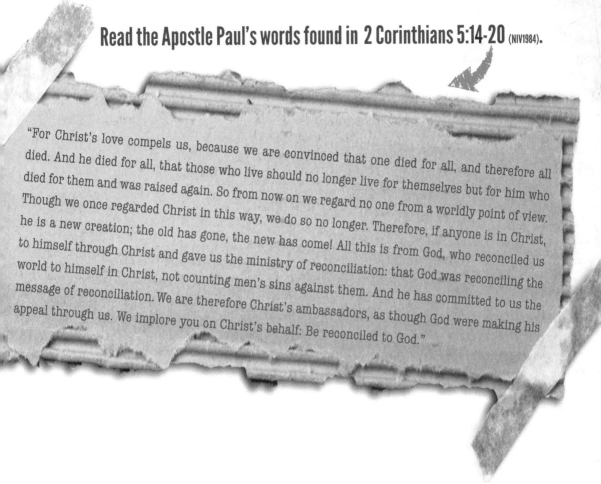

"For Christ's love compels us, because we are convinced that one died for all, and therefore all died. And he died for all, that those who live should no longer live for themselves but for him who died for them and was raised again. So from now on we regard no one from a worldly point of view. Though we once regarded Christ in this way, we do so no longer. Therefore, if anyone is in Christ, he is a new creation; the old has gone, the new has come! All this is from God, who reconciled us to himself through Christ and gave us the ministry of reconciliation: that God was reconciling the world to himself in Christ, not counting men's sins against them. And he has committed to us the message of reconciliation. We are therefore Christ's ambassadors, as though God were making his appeal through us. We implore you on Christ's behalf: Be reconciled to God."

One cannot read this passage and not feel Paul's passion for the Corinthians not only to understand the Gospel but to live as sent people because of it. This passage also reminds us why the spiritual formation of our congregation is a critical component to people understanding and seeing themselves as God's sent agents. It enables and compels them to be the Incarnate Christ, engaging, serving, and sharing Jesus with a broken and lost world. It is imperative to understanding the following truth: *People can't give away what they don't own, and people can't do what they don't know.* Sent people live like sent people because they own and understand their faith.

BASIC TENETS OF THE FAITH

As we move the congregation forward in their spiritual formation, we need to consider intentionally what aspects of faith should be included in the process. The fact is, this process does not happen without intention. We sometimes act as if people grow in their faith through osmosis; they do not. A good starting point is to begin with the basic tenets of the faith that help navigate people toward a missional heart and mindset. The following ten topics are offered as a potential curriculum—curriculum written to present a natural progression toward missional thinking and action.

1 Jesus and the human heart

Our faith is centered on the person of Jesus and His work on the cross. This teaching makes clear why Jesus matters not only for us as believers, but for the world outside our walls as well. The reconciliation that Jesus carried out through His crucifixion made redemption possible. Now, the Apostle Paul teaches that the ministry and message of reconciliation has been passed down to us as ambassadors, witnesses, missionaries, sojourners, and friends.

2 God's relentless pursuit

Understanding who God is can be a confusing, consoling, contradictory, condemning, complicated, and convoluted concept for different people. At the core of the Christian faith lies the belief of a just God whose unending love causes Him to relentlessly desire and pursue engaging us. For many folks in and outside of the church, this God of relentless pursuit is a contradiction to their perception of who God is and how they see Him being lived out through the lives of many others. It is imperative that we paint the picture, through spiritual formation, of a God whose compelling love causes Him to relentlessly pursue a relationship with us. It is a love story that never ends because God's all-encompassing love will not allow it to.

The Bible

Many people today find it difficult to see the Bible as a relevant book and not some archaic piece of literature. Honestly, tell someone who has never read the Bible, to read the book of Leviticus—they will find it has no personal connection at all. It's a difficult book even for those of us who have some faith experience; however, when people grow and begin to see the Word as living—not mundane; as transforming—not irrelevant; then life change is a natural progression. The key is to enable people to explore, decipher, and take hold of truths found within its pages.

The Holy Spirit

Plain and simple, the purpose of the Holy Spirit is to live through us, enabling us to share the love of Christ boldly with people we come in contact with every day. Many, even today, lack an understanding and a practical application of Who and what the Spirit is. People hesitate to take their faith outside the walls simply because they don't understand that the Holy Spirit can empower them to do so. Perhaps we in the body of Christ have not taught or been taught enough about this critical topic. This lesson is a commitment to make certain the Holy Spirit's power is available to every believer.

5 Intimate conversations with God

Do you ever wonder how we can make persistent prayer a more integral part of our daily lives? What if a believer came to the place where ongoing prayer was just part of the fabric and DNA of who she or he was? In the Gospel of Luke, Jesus instructs His disciples about this very concept. As we move outside our walls, these intimate conversations with God will be a necessity to sustain our efforts. It is not about simply asking God to bless our efforts, but asking God for clarity as to what our efforts should be and joining Him in His work. We begin through intimate conversations with God and the realization that those conversations must never end. As we move outside our walls, these intimate conversations with God will be a necessity to sustain our efforts.

6 Faith: the X-factor in everyday life

How do we enable faith to become the X-factor in our everyday lives? Missional people live as if God is the determining factor in their relationships, occupation, and vocation. In any and every situation, they believe God is present and active as they seek to be the tangible hands and feet of Jesus within their communities. God's Word grants us insight as to how we can live this faith everyday.

7 The integrity of how I live my life

Two key factors determine the influence of a believer's life: character and integrity. You see, those who are watching us and evaluating our faith really want to know if Jesus matters in the way we live, and if we are who we say we are in our faith. In 2 Thessalonians, Paul gives us clear examples of how we should live our lives in a manner that wins the respect of those inside and outside the walls. Moral authority cannot be valued enough as a key influencer in a believer's life. In fact, without it, the voice of our faith becomes silent.

Doing good for the cause of Jesus

Never has it been more important for the body of Christ to proclaim and demonstrate the love of Christ to a hurting and needy world. We are engaging a culture that is not moved by extravagant displays, but is longing for genuine, sincere, and tangible faith—the kind experienced when believers become the tangible hands and feet of Jesus in the lives of others. Jesus said, "Let your good deeds shine out for all to see, so that everyone will praise your heavenly Father" (Matthew 5:16 NLT). This is not rocket science—it's not hard to do. It is about having a faith that compels us outside our walls to do good things for the cause of Jesus.

Building Kingdom relationships

Do you believe God desires to expand His Kingdom through every believer's life? The answer to that question is a re-sounding yes. I also believe God desires to expand His Kingdom by the way we build relationships with others in the normal routine of life. There is nothing super-human that we have to accomplish, or some exotic place we must travel to. We make this Kingdom difference by doing what the Apostle Paul refers to in 1 Thessalonians 2:12 (NIV1984), by living *"lives worthy of God."* Sound intimidating? It's not. It is simply learning to put into practice some simple tips that Paul shares with us in 1 Thessalonians. It is about being ourselves and believing God can do extraordinary things through ordinary people like us.

"Let your good deeds shine out for all to see, so that everyone will praise your heavenly Father."

(Matthew 5:16 NLT)

10 The power of story

The two most powerful things you will ever share for the sake of Jesus are your life and your story. No one can argue with either of them. Your life is an example of how your faith intersects with reality. Your story is an example of how a living Savior changed a human being. First John 1:1 states that we proclaim to others what we have seen, heard, and touched. Learning to communicate what our life was like before Jesus, how we came to know Jesus, and what life is like after committing ourselves to Him, is what the Lord has called each of us to share. That is the simplicity and power of our story.

The spiritual formation process is best done one-on-one or in small group settings, where individuals pour their lives into another's. This happens when people have shared enough of life to engage in intimate community—not by chance, but by intent does this community and sharing take place. It is not an overnight process, but requires time, effort, and love.

NAVIGATING THE JOURNEY

Changing the Culture

- As a leadership team, take a two-day retreat and process the Root Cause Analysis six-step template on page 42.

- It is critical that time be spent in fasting and prayer before beginning this part of the journey.

- Ask others not involved in the retreat to be praying for the team during the gathering.

- To make the team's time as productive as possible, consider inviting a facilitator to guide this time.

- Make certain the pastor and facilitator have adequate time to exchange personal expectations/ideas before the retreat begins.

- Before the retreat, determine the detail person best qualified to follow through on the plan created. Remember, a dream without action is only a dream, but a dream *with* action becomes reality.

- As you make your way through the different steps, please refer back to the questions suggested for each one on page 43.

- Remember to assign responsibilities to people and target completion dates for each action identified.

- Define what measurements, methods, and time will be used to assess each of your actions and strategies.

Thinking about Spiritual Formation

What percentage of your congregation has a comfort level in taking and living their faith outside the walls?

0%_____100%

What spiritual formation/discipleship tools are currently being used effectively in your congregation?

_____

_____

_____

Four Critical Questions

- What discipleship materials best fit your congregation?
- Who will lead the spiritual formation process?
- What delivery system best fits your congregation?
- Who will you pour your life into?

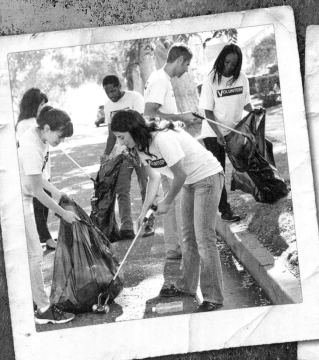

ENGAGING THE COMMUNITY

Please note: At some point, knowledge-based discipleship must transition into action-oriented followership.

"Spiritually you do not belong to the world. And this is precisely why you are sent into the world. Your family and friends, your colleagues, your competitors, and all the people you may meet on your journey through life are searching for more than survival. Your presence among them as the one who is sent, will allow them to catch a glimpse of the real life."[23]

(Nouwen, 2002)

"Congregations that understand the realities of the change taking place around them are shifting the target of their ministry efforts from church activity to community transformation."[24]

(McNeal, 2003)

The points on the previous page stress the necessity of action. A congregation can be discipled, grow spiritually, and develop a wonderful plan and strategy; however, unless a congregation engages their community with the tangible love of Jesus, it is all for nothing. Congregations must sense that God has strategically placed them in their current location for a purpose. It is not by chance but by divine placement that God has gifted, called, and positioned His people in their place of ministry. There are two truths the missional church must believe:

 Every congregation is called to be a spiritual influence and presence in the community in which it resides.

 Every life represented in every congregation has the opportunity to care for another in the name of Jesus.

In the missional church, believing truth is not enough. As God's sent people, we are compelled to act on truth; therefore, the critical question for us is this:

What must we do to engage our communities for the sake of Jesus?

To better understand how this question might be answered, let's focus on the life of Jesus and review some principles that guided His ministry. John 4 shares the story of Jesus meeting the Samaritan woman at the well. Our Lord's impact was so great it transformed not only the Samaritan woman, but a city as well. Notice that Jesus intentionally did some things that other people didn't, wouldn't, or couldn't.

FIRST JESUS WENT WHERE OTHERS DIDN'T

So [Jesus] left Judea and returned to Galilee. He had to go through Samaria on the way. Eventually he came to the Samaritan village of Sychar. John 4:3-5 (NLT)

Jesus' route to Galilee is interesting, to say the least. No upstanding religious Jew would have made his way through Samaria in order to get to Galilee. So despised were the Samaritans that Jews referred to them as "unclean dogs." The tension and disgust between the Jews and Samaritans could be traced through history, all the way back to 1 and 2 Kings, which took place around 700 BC. Talk about holding a grudge!

Jesus did not make His way to Samaria because there was no other route. There were *many* more popular routes taken by Jewish folks. And, evidently, His particular journey was not due to a time crunch. Jesus ends up spending two extra days in Samaria to be with these people.

No, Jesus made His way to Samaria for one compelling reason: the people were spiritually broken and lost. In doing so, Jesus went to people who were ostracized, minimalized, and criticized by most of the upstanding religious folks that made up His community. Also, He modeled a vivid example—our Savior went where others wouldn't go in order to reach the broken and lost, and He was constantly reminding His disciples and others of this intent. In Luke 5:30-32 (NLT), the writer states, *"But the Pharisees and their teachers of religious law complained bitterly to Jesus' disciples, 'Why do you eat and drink with such scum?' Jesus answered them, 'Healthy people don't need a doctor—sick people do. I have come to call not those who think they are righteous, but those who know they are sinners and need to repent.'"*

Jesus had a divine understanding of why He was brought to this earth—to reach a lost and broken world. Notice the different perception Jesus and the religious leaders of His day had regarding people. The religious leaders referred to the people Jesus engaged as "scum." Jesus perceived them as struggling and having needs. Too many times, good Christian people have the same critical, judgmental attitudes and perceptions as the religious leaders of Jesus' day. These perceptions and attitudes have kept us from taking the love of Christ to those seen as the outcasts and the ostracized.

Congregations who have the desire to be missional must at some point come to grips with the following questions:

Will we be broken enough by the things that break God's heart to get outside these walls and go where other people won't?

Will we perceive broken and hurting people as bothersome, or will we see them as people of value who need the wholeness of Christ?

A prime example of these mindsets is being lived out through a congregation in the Midwest. The women's ministry of that church shows unconditional love to the dancers of their city's erotic dance clubs. Twice a month an evening meal is delivered to the women at the club(s) by women who serve in this ministry. They spend time listening, caring, loving, and building relationships with each dancer.

To show their love in a more tangible way, the women once sponsored a baby shower for a pregnant dancer. The response from the church was tremendous, and the impact on the young woman was life changing. She is no longer dancing, but slowly turning her life around.

Please know the congregation that makes its way to the broken will chart a very different course than the norm. Just as Jesus did in John 4, we will be called to go where other people won't. Our focus will transition from ourselves, to meeting the needs of the broken within our community. The transition from attractional to missional calls us to see ourselves as sent people. Sent people have a deep understanding that they are called to something bigger than a local church building and the ground it rests on.

They see themselves as Kingdom workers and give themselves to showing evidence of the greater Kingdom to the community where they reside.

SECOND, JESUS POSITIONED HIMSELF WHERE OTHERS WOULDN'T

Jacob's well was there; and Jesus, tired from the long walk, sat wearily beside the well about noontime. Soon a Samaritan woman came to draw water. John 4:6-7 (NLT)

Notice that Jesus positions Himself at the well at a peculiar time of day—especially for that given place. The text informs us that it's noon, in the heat of the day, and a Samaritan woman comes to the well.

Now, right away, we know something is wrong with this picture by information John has shared with us. The woman is at the well at noon, and no other "normal" woman is going to be at the well at that time. In Jesus' day the well was a social gathering place. Traditionally, women gathered water from the well very early in the morning or very late in the evening. They did this to miss the heat of the day. In many ways this was more than a domestic duty, but a time of connection and engagement.

That was not the case for the woman noted in the text. She came to the well at a time when she would be alone and could avoid the other women. In verse 18, Jesus tells her and us why; her lifestyle has taken her through five marriages, and the man she is currently living with is not her husband. To put it plainly, she was

seen as damaged goods and shunned by all the other women. She didn't have to go to the well to be reminded of that. She had determined that it was simpler to go to the well at noon, so she didn't have to hear the whispers or endure the judgmental looks. By going at noon, she could simply avoid everybody and not have to deal with the rejection and pain she was accustomed to. She had learned her lesson well.

It would have worked too, but something unusual happened—Jesus showed up. What a powerful example of the compelling love of Christ. Jesus went where no one else would go and positioned Himself where others wouldn't because He wanted to meet a woman that nobody else wanted to meet.

From what we read and understand about Jesus, positioning Himself to be around outcast people was nothing new for Him. Lepers, adulterers, prostitutes, tax collectors, invalids, the chronically ill, blind folks, and even the demon possessed seemed to touch His life on a regular basis. In fact, this was one of the greatest criticisms of Jesus:

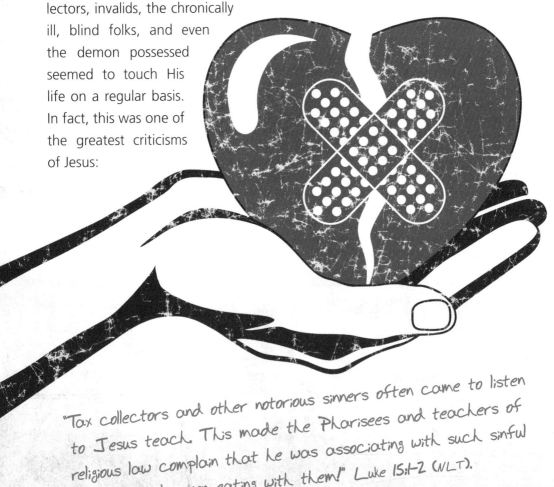

"Tax collectors and other notorious sinners often came to listen to Jesus teach. This made the Pharisees and teachers of religious law complain that he was associating with such sinful people—even eating with them!" Luke 15:1-2 (NLT).

Jesus' compelling love for the broken and lost continually enabled Him to interact, care for, and build relationships with people others would not have. Now, unless a congregation hears this truth, owns this truth, and externally lives out this truth, they will not position themselves where others won't. They will be satisfied with the status quo and position themselves in comfortable and suitable places. That congregation will spend most of its time, most of its resources, and most of its efforts, doing activities within the walls that define its existence.

But if they capture this truth and internalize it in their hearts, then they will feel compelled to live out their faith differently. They will not only go to places others won't, they will engage and serve those who are ostracized, minimalized, and criticized. Sent people do this for one reason and one reason only—we are called to be servants of our Lord Jesus.

In truth, we need to be reminded that servanthood and selflessness were the pillars on which the New Testament church was built. Again, we are not building on something new, but returning to something old. These pillars are old in the sense that they take us back to the foundations of the Church—not old in the sense that they are obsolete. In fact, the freshness of servanthood and selflessness gives congregations today more opportunities to minister than can be imagined. They are fresh today because they are an antithesis to the consumerism that drives our world and even some congregations. They are fresh today because they give credibility and proof to the selfless love we profess. Servanthood and selflessness are the foundation upon which the missional congregation rests.

Pastor Cho leads one of the largest congregations in the world. He always instructs his parishioners who are questioned about why they are serving others to respond in this way: "I am a disciple of Jesus. I am serving Him by serving you because that is what He came to do."

They will not only go to places others won't, they will ENGAGE and SERVE those who are OSTRACIZED MINIMALIZED and CRITICIZED.

Jesus' words in Matthew 25 remind and instruct us as to *who* we are called to serve:

"For I was hungry, and you fed me. I was thirsty, and you gave me a drink. I was a stranger, and you invited me into your home. I was naked, and you gave me clothing. I was sick, and you cared for me. I was in prison, and you visited me."

Then these righteous ones will reply, "Lord, when did we ever see you hungry and feed you? Or thirsty and give you something to drink? Or a stranger and show you hospitality? Or naked and give you clothing? When did we ever see you sick or in prison and visit you?"

And the King will say, "I tell you the truth, when you did it to one of the least of these my brothers and sisters, you were doing it to me!"

Matthew 25:35-40 (NLT).

One congregation discovered the joy of missional ministry as a result of deep disappointment. In the 80s the church bought forty acres outside of town, on which to construct a new building where all the facility would be on one level with plenty of parking, room for baseball fields, and the opportunity to leave the decaying inner city where its building was located. Due to many factors, the dream never became a reality. As a result, God began to work in the hearts of congregational members, and they began to see that the very location they were intent on leaving was filled with opportunities for missional living.

Today the church sponsors several annual events designed to serve their community for the Lord.

Wednesday nights during the school year, kids and parents are fed a meal, the kids are tutored, and then join in midweek programs.

During the week-long Vacation Bible School program, workers, kids, and parents are fed a meal each night before the program begins.

➡️ The church's youth group, during the summer months, spends Wednesday nights at a nearby park, building relationships with the kids while playing kickball.

➡️ Ladies from the church have built relationships with women in the neighborhood and out of this neighborhood Bible studies have begun.

➡️ In the fall, the church sponsors a Harvest Festival, where everything is free—food, games, horse rides, cakewalks, face-painting.

➡️ During the Thanksgiving meal that members of the church fix and serve to the neighborhood, coats, gloves, hats, and scarves are made available for those who need them.

While the death of the dream was difficult to take at the time, there is no doubt that God's plan for the church has turned out to be a great blessing to the church and to the neighborhood.

THIRD, JESUS GAVE WHAT OTHERS COULDN'T

Jesus said to her, "Please give me a drink." He was alone at the time because his disciples had gone into the village to buy some food. The woman was surprised, for Jews refuse to have anything to do with Samaritans. She said to Jesus, "You are a Jew, and I am a Samaritan woman. Why are you asking me for a drink?" Jesus replied, "If you only knew the gift God has for you and who you are speaking to, you would ask me, and I would give you living water." John 4:7-10 (NLT).

When the woman came to the well, Jesus did the strangest thing. He asked her for a drink of water—strange because in doing so He broke several of the social rules for a Jewish man.

First, He spoke to a woman. No upstanding Jewish man (specifically no religious teacher) would have spoken to any single woman, particularly at that place.

Second, He touched something unclean. Notice, Jesus didn't have a bucket and He had forgotten His Starbucks® cup. He would have to drink from her bucket or her ladle. In doing so, something unclean would touch His hand and mouth, therefore, making Him spiritually unclean, according to Jewish law. In her confusion she asks, "Why would You ask me for water?" The answer for Jesus is really plain and simple: It gave Jesus the opportunity to give her what no one else could, His living water.

Notice how Jesus directs the conversation toward the spiritual. He is not only there to engage her and befriend her. Those two things are critically important for missional people, and credibility through relationships is a critical platform needed to share our faith with others. Yet, as we have all witnessed, some have tried sharing their faith without earning the right to do so. The result? We are most times speaking, sometimes yelling, but no one is listening.

Jesus is there to engage and befriend her, to share with her the new life that is possible through Him. It is important that we recognize the same is possible for us. We are called to do what Scot McKnight refers to as gospeling—taking the opportunity to verbally proclaim our faith by telling our story to another[25] (2012). You

> THE ANSWER FOR JESUS IS REALLY PLAIN AND SIMPLE: IT GAVE JESUS THE OPPORTUNITY TO GIVE HER WHAT NO ONE ELSE COULD, HIS LIVING WATER.

see, it is not enough to just love and care for another person. At some point we must be willing to share the life-changing news that has been shared with us, just as Jesus did with the woman at the well. In essence, we must be willing to do the same as we give away that which has been given to us. We must be willing to go gospeling.

There are multiple reasons that we grow in our faith and there are reasons we get outside our walls. But none are more important than caring for another human being and spiritually sharing with him or her what no one else can give. The greatest need in this woman's life was not water, but for someone to engage her as a human being of worth, and at some point share with her the potential of new life in Christ. That is true for every person you will ever engage and care for in the name of Jesus.

John goes on to explain one other critical component and what happened because of Jesus' actions. *"Many Samaritans from the village believed in Jesus because the woman had said, 'He told me everything I ever did!' When they came out to see him, they begged him to stay in their village. So he stayed for two days, long enough for many more to hear his message and believe"* John 4:39-41 (NLT).

The principle of continued presence

I love the phrase John uses in verse 41, when he notes that Jesus stayed *"long enough for many to hear his message and believe."* In regard to importance, few things can re-place the ministry of presence—the factor that speaks genuine care and concern for another individual. It conveys the notion that one person values another to the extent that she or he gives time to the initiative. Continued presence gives credibility because others are able to see if someone's faith is genuine or if they are present only for the personal glory.

One life sent touched another life... and ultimately changed a city for eternity's sake.

Finally, continued presence makes a lasting difference. Listen to what John writes in verse 42: *"Then they said to the woman, 'Now we believe, not just because of what you told us, but because we have heard him ourselves. Now we know that he is indeed the Savior of the world.'"* In this instance, one life sent touched another life, which touched another life, which touched another life and ultimately changed a city for eternity's sake.

It is so important that congregations find ministries that offer them a continued presence within the community. So many times we do projects that have very little continued presence. It is difficult to build credibility and make a lasting difference when continued presence is not a part of the equation. Imagine what Mother Teresa's legacy might have been had she only stayed a day in Calcutta. The difference between a project and a presence is like the difference between a breath and a lifetime.

There is a group of men in our congregation who have taken the idea of presence and begun living it out. The ministry is called **MPJ1:27**, and stands for Madison Park, James 1:27. James 1:27(NLT) as a text instructs, "*Pure and genuine religion in the sight of God the Father means caring for orphans and widows in their distress and refusing to let the world corrupt you.*" MPJ1:27 entails a cluster of four men going to the homes of widows and single moms two Saturdays a month for two hours of work and relationship building. Every month those same men are present and engaged in that woman's life. It has been amazing to see the difference these men have made in home improvements, but more so in the personal lives of all involved. The men counsel, encourage, and walk alongside the women they have chosen to invest in. This type of difference and influence would not have been possible if continued presence had not been intentional.

As we close this chapter on engaging the community, imagine what might happen if 50% of your congregation would live their lives as God's sent people on a regular basis. What if they were willing to go where others didn't and engage people that others wouldn't? What if they equipped themselves to give away what only a believer can—the life-changing power of Jesus? Imagine if they did that every week in your community, on a continual basis. Imagine if they stayed long enough to make an eternal difference. What might happen for the Kingdom's sake and in the lives of others? The difference can be life changing, for both your congregation and those you care for in the name of Jesus.

NAVIGATING THE JOURNEY

Transitioning into action-oriented followership

On a scale of 1 – 10, how would you currently evaluate the spiritual influence and presence your congregation has in your community and why?

High 1—2—3—4—5—6—7—8—9—10 Low

_____

_____

_____

_____

Many congregations find it difficult to think outside themselves. Set aside time, as a collective whole, to brainstorm together and list new opportunities that may be on the horizon.

As you do, let the following questions guide your discussion:

Where can you go that other people don't?

_____

_____

_____

Who can you engage and care for that other people won't?

_____

_____

_____

What will you do to have a continued presence?

_____

_____

_____

As you reflect on the list of the who, what, and where, remember that all congregations need some early victories in the process. Success _does_ lend itself to success. For that reason, don't try to change the whole world in a week, just help your people succeed at serving others one day at a time.

With that thought in mind, let's go through an exercise utilizing the Effort-Impact Grid.

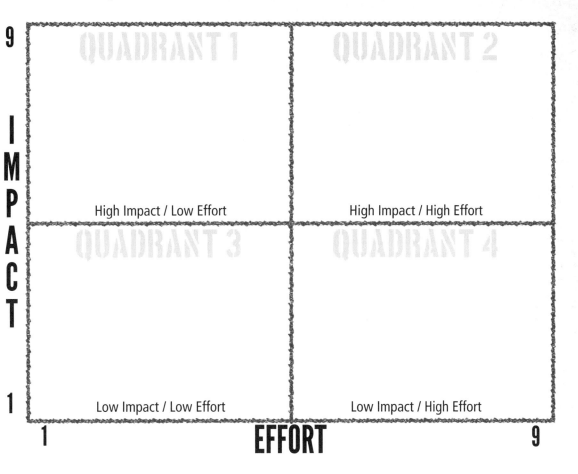

Steps to follow:

1. Make a list and number all your ideas.

2. Determine which quadrant each idea fits.

3. Place the number of the idea inside the appropriate quadrant.

4. Focus on the ideas listed in Quadrant 1.

5. Out of those ideas, pick the top 2 or 3 as the best low-lying fruit

6. Remember: do not believe _your_ idea is the only way _we_ should go.

Now, as you begin to focus and set into place new ministries, answer the following questions before you take any action:

Who will lead it? (Preferably not the pastor)

_____

What is the purpose?

_____

_____

What resources are needed?

_____

_____

What is the recommended action plan?

_____

_____

_____

PERSONAL TRANSFORMATION

Let Jesus reconfigure your life
in such a way that He interrupts
the routine in order to help
touch and heal the broken.

The transformation of any congregation is directly tied to the personal transformation of the people who make up that congregation. The Day of Pentecost's phenomenal impact on the New Testament Church was in direct correlation to the Spirit's impact on individual lives. Acts 2:4 (GW) states, *"All the believers…began to speak in other languages as the Spirit gave them the ability."* In the same way, the Spirit's power anointed Peter's sermon, and more than three thousand people were added to the church. In Acts 10, we read how two men, Peter and Cornelius, responded in obedience to God's touch on their individual hearts, and it led to the transformation of a household and then the entire New Testament church. Therein lies a fact that we must grasp: God transforms individuals on His way to transforming congregations.

> **Believers need to realize the journey begins in each of our hearts first.**

For any congregation to be transformed missionally, believers need to realize the journey begins in each of our hearts first. As the Spirit moves us, we look beyond our own congregation to the greater view of God's Kingdom around us. We all work in the Kingdom's vineyard, and that vineyard is larger than any plot of soil on which an individual congregation sits. Our part of the vineyard is the community in which we reside, and our task is to expand the Kingdom by being the hands and feet of Jesus in that community.

For this transformation to begin individually, there are some personal traits that must take root in us. As these traits take shape and become part of our spiritual DNA, our actions are also influenced by who Christ is calling and shaping us to be. Passion creates action. When the Holy Spirit begins to impassion our hearts regarding the following traits, then our actions will follow. By releasing our passions and actions, the process of transformation and Kingdom impact takes root. Ponder the following traits and define where they fit, or *if* they fit into your current life routine:

COMMIT YOURSELF TO CARE FOR ANOTHER

"Don't be selfish; don't try to impress others. Be humble, thinking of others as better than yourselves. Don't look out only for your own interests, but take an interest in others, too."

Philippians 2:3-4 (NLT)

All of us are selfish. This innate quality resonates inside each of us. We are not proud of it; we spend a great deal of time trying to cover it up, and, whether we like to admit it or not, succumb to it on a fairly regular basis. But what if something happened; what if this man Jesus touched us in such a deep way that His love and compassion for others enabled us to get over ourselves? What if our lives moved from living life to acquire stuff, to living our lives in order to have *meaning*? Before these steps can take place, some inner adjustments need to happen. I call them transformational truths.

TRANSFORMATIONAL TRUTH #1

One of the greatest gifts God ever gives is when we realize that life is bigger than us, when we move to the point that we are not consumed with ourselves. This is the point when the circumference of our lives quits revolving around the singular factor of one. I have found that many times this takes place in seasons or periods of brokenness. That is one of the beauties of brokenness, it grants us a moment or a reason to reassess our lives concerning what truly matters. It enables us to move beyond the all-consuming notion of self and focus on how we can bless and make a difference in the lives of others. When this happens to individuals, they begin to redefine their means and minutes and begin using them to help care for and give meaning to others.

When an individual and a congregation commit themselves to care for others,

TRANSFORMATIONAL TRUTH #2

they will exponentially expand their influence and impact for the Kingdom's sake. The reason for this exponential expansion is that God divinely blesses that which is not selfish and self-centered. Notice what Paul writes about the Macedonian church: *"Out of the most severe trial, their overflowing joy and their extreme poverty welled up in rich generosity"* 2 Corinthians 8:2 (NIV1984).

Please understand, the church in Macedonia was undergoing severe testing. Believers were enduring physical persecution and financial disaster as a result of their faith. Yet, Paul states, *"Out of this...their overflowing joy and their extreme poverty welled up in rich generosity."* Take a moment and really think about the equation Paul sets before us. It makes no common sense.

SEVERE TRIALS + OVERFLOWING JOY + EXTREME POVERTY = RICH GENEROSITY

The equation begs us to ask the question: what enabled them to overcome their "extreme poverty" (to hit rock bottom, down to the lowest depths)? It was their "overflowing joy" (a superabundance of an exceedingly great measure of joy). Their joy had become bigger than the circumstances of their lives. Why? Because they found meaning in serving and sharing with others what Jesus had given them. The result was they moved from being inwardly concerned for their lives to outwardly caring for others.

A consistent trait in the lives of missional people is that they commit a portion of their lives to caring for and sharing with other people. They realize Jesus has blessed them, and they are committed to sharing that blessing with others. They do not wrestle with the concept that the church exists to meet their needs and serve their interests. Their joy and the recognition of the grace poured out on them transcend the natural tendencies that self and selfishness bring out in us. As a result, they are impassioned and empowered by the Spirit to care for another. In doing so, their lives are transformed into vessels that God divinely uses. As this transformation takes place, their capacity to influence and impact the Kingdom grows also.

SEE THE KINGDOM POTENTIAL OF EVERYDAY LIFE

"A Kingdom life lived on mission is really about living ordinary, everyday life in your community, with great Gospel intentionality."[26] (Halter and Smay, 2009)

I love this quote from Halter and Smay's book because it leads me to quit looking for the extraordinary and realize that God presents significant ministry opportunities in the ordinary routine of life. The problem is that few people ever pause to intentionally notice the Kingdom potential they encounter on a daily basis. It is amazing how God coordinates the people, places, and circumstances of the ordinary to open the way for exceptional Kingdom engagement to take place.

This is not natural, however, for those who make up the Western church. We have been taught that Kingdom is related to a building and not the natural flow of life. In other parts of the world, the Gospel is growing rapidly because the natural progression of the Gospel has been built on a viral approach—one life touching another and not dependent on brick and mortar. This is a difficult mindset to break because it is all many of us have ever known. Yet, with some coaching and intent, Kingdom opportunities can be seized and taken advantage of. The following are some simple steps that can enable us to recognize and take hold of the opportunities placed along our everyday paths:

FIRST, become **spiritually sensitive** in your everyday **life.** Whether you know it or not, you come in contact with people who do not know Jesus and need His love on a daily basis. In fact, these encounters become so routine we often give them little thought. People, like the bank teller we always go to, the minimart cashier, the secretary at the office, fellow workers and neighbors who live down the street are overlooked opportunities for sharing the Gospel.

God in His great providence strategically places us in different people's lives to make a Kingdom difference; we simply need to be more spiritually aware of those we interact with. You see, we are most effective in representing Jesus when we are simply being ourselves. You don't have to be somebody you're not. You don't have to memorize half of the New Testament or be a Greek scholar. Just be who you are in your everyday life and intentionally notice the people around you.

SECOND, become intentional in building relationships with people. For some, this step just caused a rapid heartbeat and sweaty palms. Do yourself a favor and *chill*. No one is asking you to be anyone but you. Trust that God desires to use you in the lives of others, take the initiative to break the ice, and start the process of getting to know them. *The first thing to do is get to know a person's name. Everybody wants to be known by somebody, and people appreciate when someone cares enough to call them by name.*

Over time, as you build a relationship and genuine trust, ask sincere questions about who they are and how they are doing; then listen intently. Nothing shows more respect and value than when one person takes the time to listen to another. Follow up those conversations on specific situations by asking questions—this demonstrates that you really did listen. Remember those situations in your personal prayer time, and simply share with the person, "I will be praying for you." Believe it or not, people are not averse to you praying for them. They just appreciate that you care enough to pray.

Continue to be available and present in their lives. The greatest attribute any of us bring is our availability to be used. The same is true for a friend. Be available in another person's life on a regular basis, making time at some point in your week for him or her. Don't overdo it or constantly be sharing the Four Spiritual Laws. Just build a sincere, genuine relationship, and let it become a natural part of your life. Again, don't try to be somebody you're not.

THIRD, live your life with integrity and character.

Please read this section carefully. Our impact and influence are greatly diminished, and sometimes even nullified, when our actions do not reflect the faith we profess on a daily basis. The relationships we build for the sake of Jesus, and the crux of all healthy and meaningful relationships, are built on trust and truth. People outside the faith don't care if we have all the answers; in fact, they get tired of canned answers regarding faith. But, they absolutely care that we are who we say we are. If we profess to be followers of Christ, then by all means let us live out the teachings of the Jesus we profess. Titus 2:7 (NLT) challenges us in this way, *"And you yourself must be an example to them by doing good works of every kind. Let everything you do reflect the integrity and seriousness of your teaching."*

Now, don't try to sound too spiritual or perfect because, let's face it, we're not. The important thing is just to be you, blemishes and all. If you have struggles, then be honest about them. Remember, integrity and character are dependent on you being honest, sincere, and real. Let people see how your faith enables you to deal with your struggles. Let them witness and understand that in every aspect of your life this man called Jesus does engage you, walk with you, guide you, and even correct you during the ups and downs. The way you live your life with the integrity and character of Jesus impacts your influence for Him dramatically. If you profess to follow Jesus, then live your life with the integrity and character of Christ. It will be the most important thing you do in that relationship.

FOURTH, **be open to talking about spiritual things.** During your discussions, you

will be amazed at how many times your conversations lead into spiritual dialogue. Don't worry about having all the answers or responding with the perfect spiritual phrase. Trust the Holy Spirit to speak through you and to use your simple words in a supernatural way. Remember, God loves these people more than you do, and He desires nothing more than to have relationship with them. Be at ease with this fact: we will never change a human heart. Yet, God has chosen to use us common human beingsas part of this life-changing process.

I must admit, I am a little nervous about sharing this step. For some people, this suggestion is like placing a guard dog on alert. They have all the lead-in questions memorized, they know multiple Gospel presentations by heart, and they are poised to bark at any unbeliever who comes within shouting distance.

In fact, I remember witnessing this first-hand as I flew back from Los Angeles to the Midwest. At that time, the airline I was using had seats that faced each other. So there we were, four people who had never met each other, sitting in our little pod of seats. After a few minutes in the air, the woman across from me clearly believed it was her mission in life to win the man next to her to Jesus before we landed in Indianapolis. Thus began the painful process of listening to her harangue this young man with well-oiled questions of the faith. To his credit, he was gracious beyond what I would have been until he had finally had enough. With face red and voice rising, he looked at her and said, "Madam, would you please be quiet!" She acted offended, while I snickered. In truth, she was offensive and, I feel fairly certain, did very little to lead this man to Jesus.

Please know this: You and I need to *earn* the right to share Christ. We do that over time as we build genuine relationships with real people. People are not meant to be a notch on our evangelism gun belts. Our role in this process is simply to be a faithful friend, and if we are, God is big enough to hold up His end of the bargain.

FIFTH, at the right point, be willing and able to share your story.

With this step, we are brought back to McKnight's encouragement to *go gospeling*. Remember, gospeling is taking the opportunity to verbally proclaim our faith by telling our story to another[27] (McKnight, S., 2012). It is believing that at some point we need to talk about Jesus, taking to heart what John wrote in 1 John 1:3 (NLT), *"We proclaim to you what we ourselves have actually seen and heard so that you may have fellowship with us. And our fellowship is with the Father and with his Son, Jesus Christ."*

Very simply, be ready to tell what Jesus has done in your life. This is a part of the spiritual formation process. One of the ways we grow in our faith is by developing a level of comfort as we share it with others. You don't have to worry about when to share—the Holy Spirit will nudge your heart at the right moment. You don't have to be slick in your presentation; again, just be yourself and tell what difference Jesus has made in your life. It doesn't have to be dramatic—it just has to be your story. It is always amazing when God anoints the common words of a person who is willing to share about His Son. You too will be amazed when God uses you to share your story.

AT SOME POINT YOU MUST ACT ON BEHALF OF OTHERS

"You are the light of the world—like a city on a hilltop that cannot be hidden. No one lights a lamp and then puts it under a basket. Instead, a lamp is placed on a stand, where it gives light to everyone in the house. In the same way, let your good deeds shine out for all to see, so that everyone will praise your heavenly Father."

Matthew 5:14-16 (NLT)

The truth is, life comes down to moments—moments when we make decisions to change the trajectory of our lives. If you have lived life long enough as a believer, you know exactly what I mean—those critical moments when you choose to leave the comfortable and step toward the unknown in order to follow God's will for your life. It happens to all of us who choose to walk the path of obedience. It happens to anyone who says to God the words of commitment that Isaiah did, *"Here am I; send me" (Isaiah 6:8).*

These are the moments of personal transformation that call us to a place of deeper trust and dependence. The common or norm will no longer suffice. A life lived out in missional form beckons us to deep waters of faith and trust. If we are to be the tangible hands and feet of Christ, we must come to the place where we do more than discuss it; we must act on it in tangible ways. During those moments, there are insights we must not only understand intellectually but must practically take hold of, if we are ever to step out and act.

Before most people step out and act, they must overcome their fear. Don't worry; everyone has some fear. The enemy's greatest tool against anyone stepping out in ministry is a five-letter word called *doubt*—an inner anxiety that causes us to believe we won't measure up, or we don't have what it takes. Even the greatest of spiritual leaders struggled with this. Nehemiah was fearful as he approached the king for permission, blessing, and provision to rebuild the wall in Jerusalem. What were His final thoughts before entering the king's presence? Nehemiah 2:2 (ESV), *"Then I was very much afraid."* Moses felt the same in Exodus 4 after God had called him to return to Egypt and set the captives free. Moses pleaded with God in Exodus 4:13 (ESV), *"Oh, my Lord, please send someone else."* Please know most people who step out in ministry or take action in the name of Christ, must first overcome their personal fear.

To accomplish that, we must ultimately replace fear with faith. Faith is that intangible which believes if God calls, then God goes with. Nehemiah overcame his personal fear when he came to the realization that God was with him or her. Nehemiah 2:8 (ESV), *"And the king granted me what I asked, for the good hand of my God was upon me."* God answered Moses' concerns regarding his inabilities and limitations with this one simple phrase in Genesis 26:3 (NLT), *"I will be with you."* The person who has been called by God does not walk alone because God walks with him or her. Remember, when Moses received his call from God, the Word informs us that he was *"on the far side of the desert"* Exodus 3:1 (NIV1984). At no point, however, was he outside the reach and presence of God, and neither are we. We can have faith that if God calls, He goes with us.

Faith also believes that if God goes with, then God will provide for the journey. Philippians 4:13 (NLT), states *"I can do everything through Christ, who gives me strength."* There are moments when we must ultimately trust God for what we do not have. If we are determined not to act until all things are perfect, it is very likely we will never act. The Apostle Paul's words in 2 Corinthians 12:9 (NIV1984), speak directly to this issue, *"But he [Christ] said to me, 'My grace is sufficient for you, for my power is made perfect in weakness.' Therefore I will boast all the more gladly about my weaknesses, so that Christ's power may rest on me."*

> **Faith also believes that if God goes with, then God will provide for the journey.**

We all have fears, we all have limitations, we all have weaknesses, and we all have shortfalls in the resources needed. There is no person in ministry who doesn't live through these struggles. Yet, in the midst of those limitations and shortfalls is a deep-seeded belief that One much greater than you and I is working on our behalf in order to bring His will to fruition. That promise is made to us in 2 Corinthians 9:8 (NIV1984), *"And God is able to make all grace abound to you, so that in all things at all times, having all that you need, you will abound in every good work."* Rest assured today, that if God calls, then God will not only go with, but God will also provide for the journey.

FINALLY, in our efforts to act on behalf of others, we must find our place of service. If we are called to be the hands and feet of Jesus, we should find practical application in our daily lives. James 2:26 (NLT) affirms this, *"Just as the body is dead without breath, so also faith is dead without good works."* James 3:13 (NLT) continues this line of thought, *"If you are wise and understand God's ways, prove it by living an honorable life, doing good works with the humility that comes from wisdom."*

The thing we don't want to do is complicate this issue. Some folks can question and process issues to the point of paralysis. If we talk about something enough, we don't have to do it. To move us past these barriers, let's answer some simple questions in an effort to stop and move past the paralysis.

First, in what areas are you uniquely gifted and impassioned? These two aspects are important because we always work best in our comfort (giftedness) area, and we always work first in the area that brings us joy and energy (passion). That is why time managers advise us to do the things we don't want to do first. If not, passion will always win out; therefore, let's discover what energizes and comes to us most easily as we look for that place of service.

second, with your gifts and passion, where can you make the greatest difference for the Kingdom? The truth is, everyone wants to make a difference and find fulfillment. In fact, I believe this notion is so strong in most of us that over time if you feel as though you are not making a difference, you will find something else to do with your life. This step may take some trial and error to finally land in your sweet spot. That's okay, because you will be doing good in Jesus' name at every stop along the way. So, step out and serve in different positions to help others. You will know in your heart and spirit when you find the right spot. It's like shopping for the right home to buy. Something will naturally click inside you when you step through the right door and you finally say, "This is home."

Finally, ask the Holy Spirit to lead and guide you in the process. Please know God so desires to use each of us in this way that His Word encourages us constantly to use our gifts in service. I love Peterson's translation in THE MESSAGE of 1 Peter 4:7-11, *"Stay wide-awake in prayer. Most of all, love each other as if your life depended on it. Love makes up for practically anything. Be quick to give a meal to the hungry, a bed to the homeless—cheerfully. Be generous with the different things God gave you, passing them around so all get in on it: if words, let it be God's words; if help, let it be God's hearty help. That way, God's bright presence will be evident in everything through Jesus, and he'll get all the credit as the One mighty in everything."* That, my friends, is what this chapter is all about.

NAVIGATING THE JOURNEY

Moving towards personal transformation

Let's begin this section by taking a personal inventory.

Please answer the following questions.

Who are the people your life connects with on a regular basis?

1. _____

2. _____

3. _____

4. _____

5. _____

6. _____

7. _____

8. _____

9. _____

10. _____

How well do you know them?

NAME	FAMILY

NEEDS I CAN PRAY FOR...	NEEDS I CAN CARE FOR...

How do you pray for them?

DAILY PRAYER GUIDE...

Pray in confidence and faith - 2 Timothy 2:3-4

Pray for spiritual sensitivity - Psalm 139:1-4

Pray for insurmountable love – John 4:7-8

Pray that barriers of the heart be torn down
2 Corinthians 10:4-5

What are your areas of giftedness and passion?

GIFTEDNESS	PASSION

Where can you make the greatest difference for the Kingdom and find the greatest fulfillment?

_____

_____

_____

_____

_____

Where are you currently ministering?

(It makes little difference what you know about yourself if you don't do something with what you know.)

_____

_____

_____

_____

_____

TELLING YOUR STORY

"The best argument for Christianity is Christians: their joy, their certainty, their completeness."[28]

—Joe Aldrich

Stories are powerful tools of communication. Our stories of God's work in our lives help others see how Jesus can give them hope and a transformed life. Below are some suggestions to help you tell your story in a concise way.

Your life before Christ (deep, unsatisfied inner need):

_____

_____

_____

_____

_____

The circumstances surrounding how you met Christ:

_____

_____

_____

_____

_____

Your life after meeting Christ (how Jesus changed your life and what that change is like):

_____

_____

_____

_____

_____

Suggestions for Sharing Your Story

➡ No two stories are exactly alike. God can and will use your own unique experiences to speak to others. Be real. Be authentic. Be yourself.

➡ Avoid using Christian clichés and jargon.

➡ Don't use your story to criticize other churches, individuals, or groups.

➡ Do not try to be too dramatic.

➡ Avoid dogmatic and controversial statements or subjects.

➡ Practice so you can share your story in three minutes or less. Practice sharing your story with another believer to feel more comfortable telling it.

➡ Before sharing your story, pray for God's divine power to make your story a part of His work in transforming another's life.

RECOGNIZE THE KINGDOM
IS **BIGGER** THAN **YOU**

See the potential
of partnerships

May the God who gives endurance and encouragement
give you a spirit of unity among yourselves as you follow
Christ Jesus, so that with one heart and mouth you may
glorify the God and Father of our Lord Jesus Christ.

Romans 15:5-6 (NIV1984)

One of John Wooden's, UCLA basketball coach, favorite quotes was this:

"It's amazing how much can be accomplished if no one cares who gets the credit."[29]
(2005)

Redeeming the world for Jesus' sake is bigger than any one person, congregation, para-church organization, denomination, or movement. Jesus' mandate in the Great Commission was meant to offer fulfillment as His global Church functions as the singular body of Christ. Please remember, Jesus has many congregations but only one Church and that Church on mission together is His instrument to redeem the world for His sake.

Herein lies one of our greatest obstacles to shared partnerships: many attractional congregations have the mindset that other congregations are their competitors, not potential partners. This is due to the fact that attractional churches have evaluated themselves based on numbers. If, on any given weekend, congregation A has more people in attendance than congregation B down the street, A wins. For this reason, we isolate ourselves, hoard knowledge, and have petty jealousies that are never spoken. God forgive us for this underlying mindset— I know in my own personal ministry it was true for far too long.

As a result, individual congregations may win the skirmishes, but the greater Kingdom loses the war. We won't say it out loud, but this notion of success is one of the underlying

Many attractional congregations have the mindset that other congregations are their competitors. NOT

principles that has misguided the Western church's fulfillment of the Great Commission and limited the Kingdom's potential for some time particularly in the current world culture and climate in which we reside.

Please know I am not a pacifist when it comes to growing the Kingdom. Some people struggle with any thoughts of number-counting within the church. I don't. In fact, I feel very strongly that we should continue *"adding to our number daily those who are being saved,"* as Acts 2:47 informs us. I have come to believe, however, the most effective way to accomplish this is by engaging our communities as the hands and feet of Christ, building sincere and genuine relationships, and partnering with other believers in an effort to fulfill the Great Commission through the Great Commandment.

Congregations face two great limitations in reaching the world for Christ today. First, the economic struggles across the globe have hit most congregations extremely hard. As a result, congregations have had to tighten their belts by reducing staff, cutting budgets, limiting outreach endeavors, and restricting missional programs. It's funny, but I have heard more than one pastor or lay leader say, "We have had to circle the wagons." Not the perfect mindset when contemplating tackling the Great Commission or penetrating your community for Jesus, but a prevalent mindset when we visualize ourselves as independent entities instead of a part of the greater whole, which makes up the body of Christ.

Second, every congregation, no matter the size, has limitations when it comes to human resources. Every person has limited physical and emotional capabilities and every congregation is made up of those kinds of people. That is exactly why Ecclesiastes 4:9-12 (NLT) instructs us to join together with others in order to overcome the obstacles of life: *"Two people are better off than one, for they can help each other succeed. If one person falls, the other can reach out and help. But someone who falls alone is in real trouble. Likewise, two people lying close together can keep each other warm. But how can one be warm alone? A person standing alone can be attacked and defeated, but two can stand back-to-back and conquer. Three are even better, for a triple-braided cord is not easily broken."*

Earlier in the book, I wrote that one of God's greatest gifts to us is the realization that life is bigger than us. In the same way, one of the greatest gifts to the Kingdom is when congregations realize that the Kingdom work within their community is bigger than any one of them has the capacity to accomplish alone. When this happens, a Kingdom mindset begins to usher itself into existence, and the limitations of a particular building, piece of property, or group of people are overwhelmed by the desire to see the greater Kingdom increase. These Kingdom congregations begin to see the potential of partnerships, and they work to discover what ministry can be done together that could never be accomplished apart.

In truth, pettiness and jealousy must be overcome if a Kingdom mindset is to take hold. Kingdom people don't care who gets the credit; their only concern is that the Kingdom goes forth. UCLA's basketball program, under Coach John Wooden, created a model program that sustained an amazing level of excellence for a prolonged period of time. One of Wooden's favorite quotes was this, *"It's amazing how much can be accomplished if no one cares who gets the credit."* That selfless mindset enabled UCLA to function as a team committed to a common vision, and the result was winning 10 national titles.

Recently, the congregation I help pastor got to be a part of this kind of partnership, which came about by change, not by intention. I was attending a prayer event and one of the pastors attending shared about his congregation's annual *Back to School Bash*. This is an event where the children who attend our public school system have the opportunity to attend a carnival, play games for tickets, and then redeem those tickets for school supplies. The pastor shared that since that event had started, it had grown from several hundred people to over four thousand, and he needed additional volunteers to make the event happen.

As I listened, it occurred to me that this was exactly the kind of opportunity that allowed a Kingdom partnership to take place. Our mission's pastor and I met the partnering pastor for lunch, and he shared that different congregations coming alongside one another had always been his dream. He contacted us later and asked if we could recruit an additional 100 volunteers. We swallowed hard and then offered the opportunity to our congregation. To our delight and excitement, we had 102 volunteers within 2 days. Some of our people were so excited they even drove by the partnering church to sign up.

A few weeks later the event took place. The park was covered with thousands of people from different ethnicities, different kinds of family units, and different socio-economic backgrounds—all playing games and winning school supplies that would not have been affordable otherwise. In the midst of all this energy and work were the volunteers. Some of them were from the partnering church, some from our congregation, and some from the public school system—all of them working together for the common cause of blessing our community. I don't think the love of Jesus looked any better than it did that day as people just loved on children they didn't know in an effort to say…we care.

BOTTOM LINE IS

that it is not about my congregation or your congregation; it is not about who gets the credit and who doesn't. Our partnership was about developing a Kingdom mindset that moves beyond pettiness, competition, pride, and ego. It is about sharing the journey, building bridges of collaboration, multiplying our resources together, and then watching the Kingdom be expanded in ways we never could accomplish alone.

THE MOMENT IS NOW!

A selfless Kingdom mindset, based on shared responsibility, greatly increases our opportunities to engage our communities as it releases the principle of multiplication. The power of multiplication, however, only takes place as we realize that the moment for action is now. Multiple arenas of resources lay dormant until someone steps forward to enlist them and call them together.

This is really what took place in the story of Esther when Mordecai confronted her in chapter 4 13-14 (NLT) with the responsibility placed before them and stated, *"Don't think for a moment that because you're in the palace you will escape when all other Jews are killed. If you keep quiet at a time like this, deliverance and relief for the Jews will arise from some other place, but you and your relatives will die. Who knows if perhaps you were made queen for just such a time as this?"*

Esther realized the responsibility set before her was a daunting task. After taking stock of the situation, she replied to Mordecai, *"Go and gather together all the Jews of Susa and fast for me. Do not eat or drink for three days, night or day. My maids and I will do the same. And then, though it is against the law, I will go in to see the king. If I must die, I must die."So Mordecai went away and did everything as Esther had ordered him"* (Ester 4:16-17, NLT).

In one simple request, Esther multiplied her prayer resources as all those voices petitioned heaven, and God worked in miraculous ways. God awakened the king in the middle of the night, so the king asked for the book of history to be brought to him. The king then turned to the exact place where the record showed that Mordecai had exposed an assassination plot against the king and thus saved his life. The next day, Haman, who thought he would be hanging Mordecai that day, had to lead Mordecai around the city on the king's horse and proclaim his greatness to all. As the people continued to pray and fast, God continued to turn Haman's plot of destruction against him until it ended in his own death. God's people were saved and a country changed because one woman asked others to join her in the spiritual battle at hand.

Did you know there are people all around you who would come alongside you in the Kingdom's work if you would only ask them? James 4:2-3 (NLT) informs us, *"You don't have what you want because you don't ask God for it. And even when you ask, you don't get it because your motives are all wrong."* What if our motives were not selfish or self-centered? What if our intentions went beyond our individual congregations and were focused only on furthering Jesus' Kingdom within our sphere of influence? Don't you think God would bless that just as He did Mordecai and Esther?

Not too long ago a congregation in our area did that and the results were inspiring. East 91st Street Christian Church is a wonderful congregation on the outskirts of Indianapolis that has a heart for the Kingdom—especially to reach the greater Indianapolis area for Christ. They helped host a worship event where other congregations were asked to join together in the middle of Indy. The response overwhelmed all involved. Here is how they described it:

God calls churches not just to be buildings, but rather bodies that serve His world. On Sunday August 8, 2010, East 91st Street Christian Church closed its campus to host Worship in the City.

The event took place at Veterans Memorial Plaza in Indianapolis, Indiana, and included a worship service led by pastors from E91, Mercy Seat Christian Church, and Response Church.

E91's pastor at the time, Derek Duncan, said, "Worship in the City is a chance to join our community in honoring God together and to serve the people of this city. We have always had a heart for serving Indianapolis, and this is just one step of many that we will continue to take to demonstrate the love of Jesus Christ to our community."

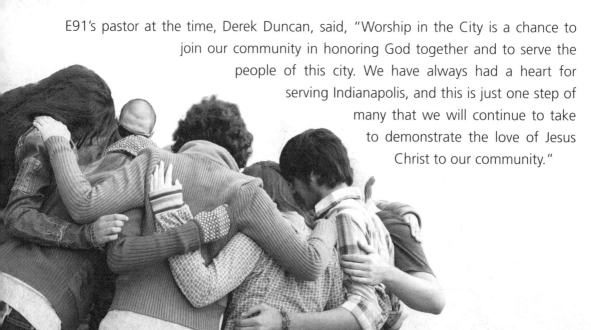

Attendance and lunch were free for anyone who wanted to participate. Members of the churches came into the city to worship with people there as one body of Christ.

While in the city, participants assisted with neighborhood cleanup and helped feed the homeless. The music was diverse, and several pastors were able to share their hearts with all who were listening. The unity among the three churches created even further unity with the churches and the people in the city.

God brought thousands of people to the event, many of whom were not members of the churches. Deb Meitzler was on staff at E91 as the senior pastor's executive assistant and helped with planning the event. She said that several thousand people were in attendance, and that it was clear God was moving.

Even during the rehearsal time, people were coming to talk with band members and staff about what they were doing and who Christ was. "It was a pretty impactful event and a good day of incredible testimonies," said Meitzler. Through a few churches going out into their community, hope was brought to thousands. (Anna Rayis, Communication Intern, June 27, 2013)

Now is the time—
the moment is here—to realize that the Kingdom is bigger
than any of us. Redeeming our communities for Jesus' sake is bigger than any one congregation can accomplish alone. But together, we can multiply our resources, our strength, and our resolve. We can come together as the larger body of Christ and accomplish more than we ever could independent of one another. The Apostle Paul exhorts the church in Romans 15:5-6 (NIV1984) to be unified in mission and ministry: *"May the God who gives endurance and encouragement give you a spirit of unity among yourselves as you follow Christ Jesus, so that with one heart and mouth you may glorify the God and Father of our Lord Jesus Christ."* It is my hope and prayer these verses will become reality for you and the congregations in your community, as you come together and realize that the Kingdom is bigger than YOU.

CONCLUDING THOUGHTS

During the writing of this book, I received a phone call at 3:00 A.M. one morning. A young man in our congregation, only 18 years old, had lost his life. I arrived at the family's home around 3:30, and the pain of that moment was almost unbearable. They are a great family who dearly love one another, and the loss of one of their two sons brought a depth of hurt I don't have words to describe. We prayed, we cried, we held each other, and we just sat together.

The truth is, there is a broken world around all of us that desperately needs this hope.

Over the next several days, we discussed hope, the cross, redemption, good and evil, God's omnipotence, and the brokenness of this world. But there was one thing that held all our conversations and hope together. It was the reality that God loved us so much that one day He chose to enter the world and our brokenness in the form of His Son. Jesus, the Incarnate God, became flesh and made His dwelling among us. Because of that action, our lives have been changed and so has our hope for the future.

The truth is, there is a broken world around all of us that desperately needs this hope. To bring this hope to the world, however, people in congregations like mine and yours will need to become the hands and feet of Jesus. This incarnate Christ will find meaning and purpose as He is lived out in practical, compassionate ways. Bigger and better programming or facilities that wow us when we enter them will not bring hope—one person touching another person, who touches another person and so on, in the name and love of Jesus will bring hope, meaning, and purpose.

This will only happen if the majority of our current congregations move from being the church caught in the middle and make their way to the land of missional living. It will not happen by chance but only by intent. It will not happen without perseverance to stay the course and passion to reach the broken and hurting. It will not happen if we are only broken by our needs and not broken by the things that break God's heart.

Here's the crazy thing:

I BELIEVE,
THROUGH THE POWER OF JESUS IT CAN HAPPEN.

I BELIEVE,
most people want their faith and actions to bless somebody else for the cause of Christ.

I BELIEVE,
we can move past our selfishness and understand servanthood is our one true calling.

I BELIEVE,
God will anoint our efforts and bless our partnerships in a way that will transform our communities.

I BELIEVE,
there is a spiritual hunger in our society today that can only be filled with the tangible, compassionate love of Jesus being lived out by His people.

I BELIEVE,
because of that spiritual hunger, the potential for Kingdom growth is exponential.

My prayer is that you believe it also—not only that you believe it, but that you will commit to making the Incarnate Jesus a reality in your congregation's DNA. May you determine and covenant as a congregation to make this journey as Christ-like people on a Christ-centered mission to fulfill a Christ-given calling.

That is why this book was written, and I close with this prayer:

Father, May the power of Your Holy Spirit anoint these words as You did the words of others on the day of Pentecost. May the result be the same, as thousands, literally hundreds of thousands, come to Your Son, Jesus, as congregations reach out to their communities, becoming the hands and feet of Jesus.

I simply ask this in the all-powerful name of Jesus, for that is enough.

Amen and Amen.

NAVIGATING THE JOURNEY

Recognize the Kingdom is bigger than YOU

Define some of the benefits and obstacles your congregation could face, entering into Kingdom partnerships.

BENEFITS	OBSTACLES

How can some of those potential obstacles be overcome?

_____

_____

_____

_____

_____

_____

_____

Who are some potential partners you might invite to come alongside you?

1. _____

2. _____

3. _____

4. _____

5. _____

What strengths and needs do you bring to the partnership?

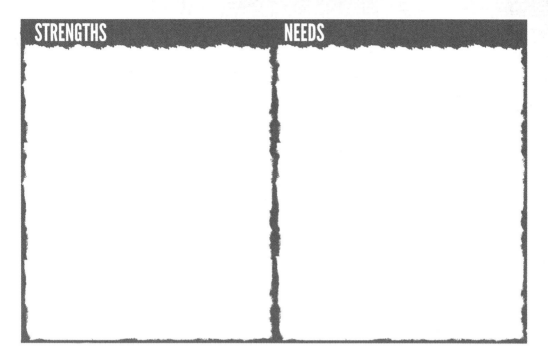

STRENGTHS

NEEDS

THE TIME IS NOW

Determine the immediate steps you need to take to make partnership a part of your congregation's DNA.

1. _____

2. _____

3. _____

4. _____

5. _____

Notes:

ENDNOTES

1   Sills, G. L., Vroman, N.D., Wahl, R.E. & Schwanz, N.T. (May, 2008). Overview of New Orleans Levee Failures: Lessons Learned and Their Impact on National Levee Design and Assessment. *Journal of Geotechnical and Geoenvironmental Engineering, 556-565.*

2   Brokaw, T. (1998), *The Greatest Generation.* New York: Random House.

3   Hamm, R. (2007), *Recreating the Church, Leadership for the Post Modern Age.* St. Louis, MO: Chalice Press, p. 90.

4   McNeal, R. (2009), *Missional Renaissance.* San Francisco, CA: Jossey-Bass.

5   Stetzer, E. (2006), *Planting Missional Churches.* Nashville, TN: Broadman & Holman Publisher, p. 28.   P.12

6   Haltar, H. and Smay, M. (2009), *The Tangible Kingdom Primer.* US: Missio Publishing, p.17.

7   Carroll, Lewis. (1866), *Alice's Adventures in Wonderland.* New York, NY, Appleton.

8   Hirsch, A. (Fall, 2008), "Defining Missional," *Leadership Journal*, Leadershipjournal.net, June 6, 2012.

9   Putnam, D. and Stetzer, E. (2006). *Breaking the Missional Code.* Nashville, TN: Broadman & Holman Publishers.

10 Doyle, A. (March 27, 2011). *County church leaders see need for growth*. The Herald Bulletin, Anderson, IN.

11 Putnam, D. and Stetzer, E. (2006). *Breaking the Missional Code.* Nashville, TN: Broadman & Holman Publishers.

12 Hirsch, A., (April 2, 2012) www.youtube.com/watch?v=Zv-Hpx-5Ye4. Last accessed April 8, 2012.

13 Ibid.

14 Lillian Russell. BrainyQuote.com, Xplore Inc, 2013. http://www.brainyquote.com/quotes/quotes/l/lillianrus197618.html, accessed October 15, 2013.

15 McNeal, R. (2003), *The Present Future, Six Tough Questions for the Church.* San Francisco, CA: Jossey-Bass, p.18.

16 Hirsch, A., (April 2, 2012) www.youtube.com/watch?v=Zv-Hpx-5Ye4. Last accessed April 8, 2012.

17 Stokes, M. E. (2009) "Inside Out: A Detailed Plan for Improving Spiritual Health at Olde Towne Community Church, Ridgeland, Mississippi." Doctorate of Ministry dissertation, Anderson University, Anderson, IN.

18 Briscoe, Brad. (2010) Missional Church Network, May 2010.

19 Ibid.

20 Hirsch, A., (April 2, 2012) www.youtube.com/watch?v=Zv-Hpx-5Ye4. Last accessed April 8, 2012.

21 Stott, John. (1979), *The Message of Ephesians*. Downers Grove, IL: Inter-Varsity Press, p.179.

22 Kinneman, D. (2012). Quote used from David Kinneman's teaching at Anderson University's chapel service. The Barna Group: Barna Research, Thousand Oaks, CA.

23 Nouwen, Henri. (2002), *Life of the Beloved. Spiritual Living in a Secular World*. New York, NY: The Crossroad Publishing Company.

24 McNeal, R. (2003), *The Present Future, Six Tough Questions for the Church*. San Francisco, CA: Jossey-Bass, p.18.

25 McKnight, S. (2012), *Is it still evangelism if there are no words*. Outreach Magazine, November/December, p. 62.

26 Haltar, H. and Smay, M. (2009), *The Tangible Kingdom Primer*. US: Missio Publishing.

27 McKnight, S. (2012), *Is it still evangelism if there are no words*. Outreach Magazine, November/December, p. 62.

28 Aldrich, J. (1981, 1993), *Lifestyle Evangelism*. Colorado Springs, CO, Multnomah Books, p. 21.

29 Jamison, S. and J. Wooden, *Wooden on Leadership: How to Create a Winning Organization*. New York: McGraw-Hill, p. 30.

Notes:

Notes:

Notes:

Notes:

Notes:

Notes: